D1606801

EMDR
THERAPY TOOLBOX

Self-help techniques to eliminate anxiety, depression, and anger and to overcome traumatic stress symptoms.
Theory & treatment of complex ptsd & dissociation to retrain your brain

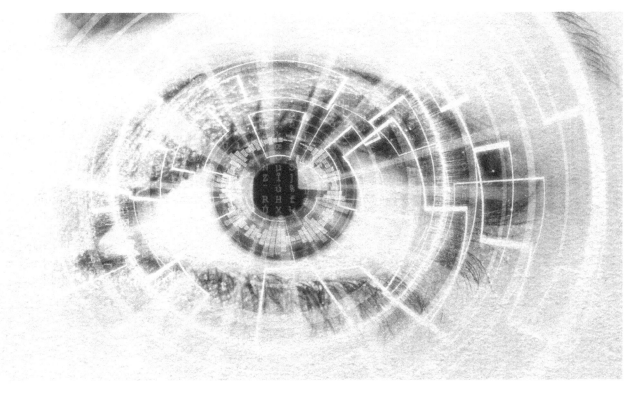

DAVID REYES

© Copyright 2019 by **David Reyes**

All rights reserved.

This document is geared towards providing exact and reliable information with regards to the topic and issue covered. The publication is sold with the idea that the publisher is not required to render accounting, officially permitted, or otherwise, qualified services. If advice is necessary, legal or professional, a practiced individual in the profession should be ordered.

- From a Declaration of Principles which was accepted and approved equally by a Committee of the American Bar Association and a Committee of Publishers and Associations.

In no way is it legal to reproduce, duplicate, or transmit any part of this document in either electronic means or in printed format. Recording of this publication is strictly prohibited and any storage of this document is not allowed unless with written permission from the publisher.

All rights reserved.

Table of contents

INTRODUCTION

Eye Movement Desensitization and Reprocessing (EMDR) is a recent psychotherapeutic technique, initially developed for the treatment of PTSD, but now used to address several clinical disorders resulting from traumatic experiences.

EMDR, as part of a comprehensive therapeutic plan, uses an eight-step procedure, with the aim of working on traumatic experiences and memories, the basis of current problems and disorders. The characteristic of EMDR is that, in order to help the patient to access and metabolize the memory, it is asked to focus on the most disturbing part of the memory and on all its aspects (images, negative cognitions, negative emotions, body sensations), while a bilateral stimulation of the eyes is induced (more or less a complete rotation per second, in a period of time ranging from 20 to 60 seconds). As the work progresses, the patient creates more adaptive material that is integrated with the traumatic memories. As a consequence, the disturbing aspect of traumatic memory is resolved, thus achieving a restructuring of the associated cognitions and a more positive and adaptive vision.

EMDR was discovered in 1987 by Francine Shapiro. One day, in fact, while walking in a forest, he began to see that some of his disturbing thoughts suddenly disappeared and that, trying to call them to mind again, no longer had the characteristic of discomfort and disturbance. He also discovered that when disturbing thoughts appeared in the mind, his eyes moved spontaneously and quickly, back and forth, following an upward diagonal. He could still notice that by calling to mind annoying thoughts and intentionally moving the eyes, they tended to lose their disturbing characteristic (Shapiro, 1995). Fascinated by her discovery, she began to devote herself to the scientific study of her intuition. In the same year, in fact, he worked on his first controlled study, published in 1989 in the Journal of Traumatic Stress. Meanwhile, in 1988, Shapiro came into contact with the Mental Research Institute (MRI) in Palo Alto, California, a research institute interested in systemic therapy.

The Institute's main focus was on the development of relationships, short term therapy and a strong openness to psychotherapeutic innovations, which led to his studies and collaboration within the Institute.

Originally EMDR was conceived as EMD, a rapid form of treatment of traumatic memories, useful for subjects with PTSD, which allowed, through eye movements, a desensitization of traumatic memories. Subsequently the technique was refined, enriched conceptually and empirically, thus transforming into EMDR, with the addition of the word "Reprocessing", as Shapiro realized that the procedure not only produced a desensitization, but also a processing of information. "During the treatment, negative emotions were replaced by positive ones, deeper insights emerged, body sensations changed, and new behaviors spontaneously appeared, along with a new sense of self. In short, trauma has been transformed into learning experiences that have quickly strengthened the person from a victim to a survivor to a healthy and robust individual. In this regard, Shapiro also reformulated the theoretical basis, talking about the Model of Adaptive Information Processing (Model AIP).

Currently, EMDR has been the subject of numerous research studies and has been recognized as an efficient and effective treatment for PTSD in civilian populations by the American Psychological Association, based on empirical evidence from a 1995 study project conducted by the Department of Clinical Psychology of the American Psychological Association. The International Society for Traumatic Stress Studies (ISTSS) has also considered EMDR to be an effective procedure for the treatment of PTSD, giving an A/B classification, where A has been assigned on the basis of 7 controlled studies that have given significant results; B, on the other hand, indicates that there is a need for more extensive studies that focus research on the comparison between the various interventions that treat PTSD. Currently these studies have been completed and EMDR, in addition to being considered the most effective treatment for PTSD, is also the one with more research to prove its effectiveness. In fact, together with CBT, it is considered the elective treatment for the PTSD (Clinical Resource Efficacy Team of the Northern Ireland Department of Health, 2003)

- Quality Institute Health Care CBO/Trimbos Institute, 2003 - French National Institute of Health and Medical Research, 2004 - American Psychiatric Association, 2004). Furthermore, EMDR is considered to be one of the three recommended methods for victims of terrorism.

The mechanism underlying EMDR is not yet entirely clear, it is suggested that cognitive restructuring and adaptive reworking take place at a neurophysiological level. According to some hypotheses, eye movements stimulate an orientation response that activates neurophysiological states that allow to inhibit fear and anxiety associated with traumatic memory. Other hypotheses report that eye movements would activate mechanisms similar to those of REM sleep, i.e. the processing of information occurring during EMDR would be similar to that occurring during REM sleep, as demonstrated by a recent study, according to which eye movements inhibit the sympathetic system, creating a situation similar to that of REM sleep. Further hypotheses suggest that the effects produced by the EMDR treatment are related to hypnotic suggestion. The hypotheses that find greater agreement are those according to which the consolidation of memories would be achieved thanks to the bilateral cooperation of the two brain hemispheres, triggered by ocular stimulation.

"In its twenty years of history, it has evolved from a simple technique to become an integrated psychotherapy approach with a theoretical model that recognizes at the base of the pathology the information processing systems of the brain and the memories related to traumatic life experiences.

CHAPTER ONE:
EMDR AND THEORETICAL BASES

Theoretical basis: The Model of Adaptive Information Processing (Model AIP)

The Adaptive Information Processing Model (AIP), adopted by Shapiro (1995), assumes that in all human beings there is an innate neurobiological function that tends towards information processing. This implies that, under normal conditions, incoming information is processed and transformed into adaptive material that functionally integrates with past experiences and information. "The information would then be stored in a system of Amnestic networks. It is believed that a network contains the individual components, thoughts, images, emotions and sensations that can be connected to the memory of the experience. Processing or re-elaboration is defined as the creation of the necessary associations, so that learning takes place once the information belonging to an event has been resolved in an adaptive way". The problems of this process may arise when the experience is not properly elaborated, and this is the case of traumatic experiences. In these cases, information processing is not adaptive, and the information remains isolated in its own neural networks and is not able to connect with other memory networks that contain more adaptive information. The possibility of integration is therefore compromised, with the consequence that the information remains enclosed in the brain in its specific form, i.e. stored as it was proven at the time of experience, with the same emotional, sensory, cognitive and physical components. Pathology is seen as the result of unprocessed and transformed experiences. Attitudes, emotions and sensations are not, therefore, simple reactions to past events, but are seen as a manifestation linked to the perception of memories stored.

"Shapiro's theory of inadequate processing of disturbing events provides an explanation of the enduring and apparently immutable resilient nature of some traumatic memories related to post-traumatic disorders. Generally, in the therapeutic field, we observe that these memories are resistant to cognitive restructuring and have difficulty being assimilated into the network of other memories of the individual. In fact, we note that the patient is only able to recall negative memories [...] because negative information is kept dysfunctional in an excitatory form and, consequently, is stimulated more easily than others". "A failure in processing ensures that negative memories remain warm and susceptible to being reactivated at any time. Consequently, regardless of the number of positive experiences that follow one another during a person's lifetime, early unprocessed events can lay the foundations for an impoverished sense of identity and self-efficiency. By using EMDR in psychotherapy, and in particular in the treatment of PTSD, it is possible to access the information stored in a dysfunctional way, going to activate the innate system that allows you to process the information. This activation can take place thanks to the procedure of the standard protocol of the EMDR characterized, in particular, by the bilateral stimulation of the eyes, with the aim of creating links between the amnestic networks and a more adaptive storage of information. The EMDR, therefore, allows to create associations between non-integrated and dissociated information, and to access the information blocked in the networks amnestic, generating new learning. In fact, disturbing information is eliminated, useful information is properly integrated and used as a guide for future behavior and decisions.

"The AIP model distinguishes EMDR from other forms of psychotherapy by the fact that it sees situations that cause discomfort in the present, simply as activators able to recall events from the past that have not been properly processed. It is thought that the current event stimulates the amnestic network, allowing negative emotions, physical sensations and stored thoughts to resurface.

Although EMDR has developed within the behavioral tradition, over time it has become a very different therapy. In fact, while in cognitive and behavioral therapies the objective is to address the patient's disorder directly, going to change the thoughts and behavior of the patient in the here and now, in the AIP model, however, the cause of the problems is not in negative cognitions, but in the memories of early situations that have been stored in a non-adaptive way. From the point of view of clinical practice, therefore, unlike behavioral therapy, taking the example of phobias, they are not treated by exposing the patient in front of the object or the situation that causes fear, but by proceeding by addressing and processing the early memories that are related to the event or the object that causes anxiety. Then we move on to the present targets, asking the patient to imagine current experiences that can trigger fear. When the patient no longer feels afraid imagining the situation, we work on a future target, imagining that we are dealing with the previous event, but without fear. "Consequently, the EMDR treatment proceeds from the inside out and deals with the inner world before using typical Cognitive Behavioral Therapy tools such as role-play experiential modeling or techniques to incorporate sets of skills that can characterize a healthy adult.

The EMDR standard protocol: tools and treatment steps

"EMDR procedures have been developed to access dysfunctional experiences stored in a dysfunctional way and stimulate the information processing system, so as to allow the transformation of information into an adaptive resolution, moving the information to a more appropriate memory system. When it is completely processed, useful information is assimilated and the structures of the individual's memory are reorganized on the basis of the new information" (Shapiro, 2011, p.17). On this basis, the protocol includes a number of useful tools for recalling and elaborating the memory. In particular, the key components of EMDR are (Greenwald, 2000):

* The repertoire of images: the patient chooses the most disturbing or, in any case, most characteristic image of the memory that best represents the negative effect on the patient.

* Negative cognition: it is not a simple description of the event, but an interpretation of the patient's opinion of himself that emerges from the memory. Some examples of the most common negative knowledge: "I'm a bad person", "It was my fault". The characteristic of this knowledge is that it persists even after the trauma and continues to reoccur throughout the patient's life.

* Positive cognition: also, in this case is not a description, but a more positive adaptive self-affirmation, and represents the goal of the treatment, that is, how the patient will see himself. Examples of the most frequent positive knowledge: "I'm a good person", "I'm safe now", "I can do it".

* The Cognition Validity Scale (COV): is a scale that allows the therapist and the patient to observe the progress made during and after the EMDR, as it gives a measure of how truthful the patient considers the positive information that you want to install with the procedure. It consists in measuring positive cognition on a scale from 1 to 7, where 1 means "completely false cognition" and 7 means "completely true cognition".

* Emotion: the patient must express the emotional reaction to the image of the memory he has chosen. Examples of most frequent emotions: fear, anger, sadness.

* The Subjective Disorder Unit Scale (SOUTH): allows the therapist and the patient to verify the progress achieved during and after the EMDR, as it indicates the intensity of the disorder perceived by the patient, and consists of measuring how intense the current negative emotion is on a scale ranging from 0 to 10, where 0 indicates "absolute absence of disorder" and 10 "disorder as intense as possible".

* Physical sensation: it is considered an integral part of the memory, since the characteristics of the amnestic traces are also preserved in the body. Affective states not properly integrated, survive in somatic states. The patient is asked to express in which part of the body he feels the physical sensation that accompanies that memory. Among the most frequent sensations we find nausea, fatigue and localized tension.

* Eye movements: the therapist induces rapid bilateral eye movements by moving his fingers at a rate of about one movement back and forth per second, at a distance of about 30-60 cm from the patient's face. If, for various reasons, eye movements are not adequate, other stimulations may be used. Eyepiece movements allow access to the souvenir-target, its processing and integration.

According to Francine Shapiro's original approach, the basic EMDR protocol consists of eight phases, each phase devoting itself to a different aspect of the treatment, although it should be remembered that each phase can have effects on several phases at the same time.

Dworkin conceptualizes the EMDR procedure in three stages, within which the eight stages are distributed:

Stage 1: Evaluation and preparation

* Phase 1: Understanding the case with regard to the trauma (history collection and treatment plan).

* Phase 2: Evaluation of the patient's capacity for emotional tolerance and awareness of physical sensations (patient preparation).

Stage 2: Active work on trauma

* Step 3: Trauma activation sequence (assessment).

* Step 4: Active trauma processing (desensitization).

* Step 5: Connecting to an Adaptive Perspective (Installation).

* Step 6: Intensive body scan.

Step 3: Closure and revaluation

* Step 7: Debriefing.

* Step 8: Reassessment.

The various stages of EMDR treatment will be explained below, following the descriptions of Dworkin:

> **Phase 1: anamnestic collection and treatment plan**

The initial phase is an important moment for the reception of the patient and for the construction of an appropriate climate of alliance and trust, because the EMDR is not something that the therapist does to the patient, but it is something that he does with him is that therefore requires collaboration and active participation. Furthermore, before active work on the trauma is started, it is essential that the patient is assessed and considered suitable for treatment.

In this phase, in fact, we try to obtain a complete clinical picture of the patient useful for implementing an adequate therapeutic plan and for formulating the objectives. In particular, it begins with a history of trauma, since it is believed that many problems experienced by patients, even if apparently do not have trauma as a central cause, can still be related to traumatic or stressful experiences. This information helps to create the context of trust necessary for processing.

The construction of the report is also fundamental and requires all the necessary time. The patient-therapist relationship starts from the first contact, and is the beginning of an attachment relationship, influenced by the first attachment relationship of the patient with the caregiver. The clinician becomes, therefore, a very important attachment figure for the patient and must be able to develop an initial understanding of who the patient is and what he is fighting against.

In addition to these aspects, it is necessary, however, to already think in terms of EMDR, working on memories and knowledge. In particular, it is useful to ask for the negative knowledge a patient has of himself and also what he would like to believe about himself once the treatment is over. This information can then be used in Phase 2.

In addition, the clinician must ask the patient for his strengths, resources and successes; many patients have internal resources that they believe they do not have, so it is important to investigate and expand them.

➢ **Phase 2: Patient preparation**

This phase starts with a presentation of EMDR, not in a technical way, but trying to explain in a simple way how it works and why it can be effective for the patient. This explanation is fundamental, because the way in which it is received is indicative and predictive for the effectiveness of the entire therapy.

It is also important to test bilateral stimulation on the patient. First of all, the most commonly used modes are presented and then the patient is given a try using a neutral image. Then it is useful to direct the work on the trauma, preparing the patient and giving him some indications on how to manage the treatment, reiterating what was said in the previous phase, that is, that the patient will have an active participation.

In the preparatory work you have to:

* inform the patient of the possibility of using protective factors, such as the "stop signal",

* describe and explain techniques for dealing with stress,

* explain the importance of noting down what happens between sessions,

* to convey the idea that irrational responses that may potentially occur during processing, are part of the normality and refer to the opening of mystic networks,

* describe the various steps of the active work on trauma and provide precise instructions regarding what will happen during the active phases.

Following patient preparation, it is important to develop a sense of security. The first step is the creation of the "safe place", an exercise that allows clinicians to understand if the patient has the ability to develop their sense of security, and the patient to install a place of security and well-being, useful for dealing with and working on difficult material.

The procedure is as follows:

* Step 1: The clinician asks the patient if he has a place where he feels safe and protected. If the patient is in difficulty, the therapist can help him by using the strategy of development and installation of resources.

* Step 2 and 3: Ask the patient to focus on the image of his or her safe place, focusing also on the description of the feelings and emotions that the image evokes, and communicating where he or she feels these feelings in his or her body. This step allows the patient to have a contact with their own internal experience related to traumatic memory.

* Step 4: After the patient has managed to find his or her own safe place, he or she can experience bilateral stimulation for the first time. In this step, the clinician asks the patient to evoke the image of the safe place and to focus on the positive feelings and sensations it arouses, paying attention to the physical sensations as well. Bilateral stimulation will be short. The therapist then asks the patient again to report whether the positive feeling has been strengthened and amplified.

* Step 5: The therapist asks the patient for a meaningful keyword that has characteristics that can be linked to the chosen safe place. Then it proceeds again with bilateral stimulation.

* Step 6: The patient independently activates the safe place by means of the keyword. This technique can be useful to you at any time during the treatment and during your life when you feel uncomfortable.

* Step 7: The patient evokes a disturbing event, and the therapist recalls the chosen keyword, asking the patient to enter the safe place.

* 8th step: the patient autonomously uses the keyword to enter the safe place.

The therapist must also help the patient to find and develop coping strategies. You can use the technique of RDI (Resource Development and Installation) that requires to evoke a positive experience, a satisfying relationship or other elements that represent strength and calm, or you can ask the patient to think of resources to be strengthened that potentially possesses or that can be developed, to be used to deal with difficult situations. The categories of resources that can be developed are:

* resources of mastery: a memory of the patient in which he was able to overcome a problematic situation, or a physical condition or a particular skill;

* relational resources: the real or fantastic image of a person or an animal that arouses in the patient protection and that have a positive role;

* symbolic resources: the memory of objects, symbols, spiritual experiences, images, figures of one's dreams, metaphors, phrases, musical pieces associated with feelings of security, strength and serenity.

Once the resource is developed, it is then installed through bilateral stimulation. Before starting the desensitization work with the patient, it is advisable for the clinician to make sure that the patient is able to successfully use some of the resources developed even in everyday situations. In fact, when the resources chosen are sufficiently internalized by the patient, they help to strengthen the self and to deal with problematic situations.

The last step of this phase is to assess whether the patient is ready to work actively on the trauma. The factors to consider are:

* coping and adaptation skills,

* emotional tolerance (and activation),

* the capacity for self-regulation (both personal and in interaction),

* affective patterns, and positive and accessible resources,

* an adequate and observant "self".

> **Phase 3: Assessment**

After the therapist, with the previous phase, has ascertained that the patient is ready for the processing of the trauma, it is possible to start what Dworkin calls "sequence of activation of the trauma". At this stage it is possible to rework the trauma and relive the traumatic past, in a current relationship, however, safe and protected. The clinician, in fact, assumes the role of co-participant.

The objective of this phase is to access traumatic memories, working in detail and comprehensively on the "souvenir-target", i.e. going to evaluate all the associated elements: the selected image, the negative cognition, the positive cognition with the VOC score, the emotion with the SOUTH score and the physical sensation. By fully activating the memory networks associated with target remembering, you can deal with the entire traumatic experience, including all related emotions and associated body sensations. To find the link between the past and the current difficulties, it is important to develop the brain's ability to process information "so that it can relate to the old trauma and reorganize the experience in a more adaptive way".

The first step is to select targets. It starts with a list of the ten worst memories related to the current difficulties, described by the patient during Phase 1.

In particular, the selection concerns two categories:

* The oldest memory, or rather the most painful memory, connected to painful emotions and negative cognitions, which is strongly associated with the patient's problem.

* The worst of these memories.

The patient, together with the clinician, will then decide which memory to use as a target. The best choice seems to be to start with one of the oldest memories that hurts now. In order for the activation sequence to begin, it is essential that the image is clear and well "in focus". In fact, the clearer the traumatic image is for the therapist, the easier it will be to focus the target and the greater the chances that the results will be long-lasting and successful.

In addition to the memories-targets found, dreams can also be valid target images. The dream, in fact, can represent a continuation of the work on the trauma in an involuntary way, and it can often appear in the interval between one session and another. In this regard, it is good to ask the patient to keep a dream diary, especially in the days following the bilateral stimulation.

Once the target image has been identified, it is necessary to deal with the negative cognition, i.e. the negative judgement that the person has with respect to himself, in relation to the selected target memory. The patient, within a safe and protected therapeutic relationship, is in a position to express aspects of himself, related to the target memory, which for a long time remained hidden. It is important that the negative judgment refers to the present, so it is advisable to include the term "now" in the question addressed to the patient. This word is used because traumatic memory is rooted in the present but is not recognized as such.

It is not always easy for a patient to express negative cognition, even if he has understood the concept and knows how to use it. In fact, even if the patient in Phase 2 understood the link between the image of the traumatic event and a negative thought, he can block himself in Phase 3, when he hears the word "now" inserted in the question. In this regard, the therapist must clarify certain points to the patient:

* to make the patient understand that he has to identify a thought, not a feeling;

* that the selected thought, even if it is linked to the past, still expresses itself in the present in old brain circuits;

* the reference to the word "now" is linked to these circuits that must be reactivated and on which it is appropriate to work;

* The clinician should remember that the patient is invaded by a negative arousal, so his explanation may be difficult to decode and follow.

After identifying negative cognition, you can work on positive cognition and VOC. Positive cognition is an important element that gives confidence and strength to the patient in dealing with his "pathology". It also allows the patient to benefit from an alternative to negative self-confidence. The VOC, on the other hand, allows us to understand how much the positive cognition of the patient is near or far from the reality of the patient.

Then the therapist asks the patient to put together the chosen image and the negative cognition, give a name to the emotions he feels and evaluate the SOUTH scale. The final moment of Phase 3 is the body scan, which consists of asking the patient to listen to their own body sensations and to report in which parts of the body they feel the emotions previously mentioned.

The success of this step allows you to move to Phase 4 and the work of desensitization. Before leaving Phase 3, it is important to re-enhance the patient's confidence in the therapist and to reiterate that the therapist is a guide and that the patient is not only faced with his or her problem, but can share it and work on it in a protected manner.

> **Phase 4: Desensitization**

Phase 4 is dedicated to the elaboration of trauma, and the desensitization of one or more memories related to the traumatic experiences of the patient. Bilateral stimulations, such as eye movements, are used in this phase, while the patient focuses on the many aspects of memory derived from the previous phases. After these first series of eye movements, the therapist asks the patient what has emerged, and continues to work with eye movements on what the patient has noticed. This goes on until all aspects of remembrance are overcome and neutralized. The demonstration is given by the scores of the scale SOUTH and VOC.

Patients who have poor emotional tolerance during the processing of trauma may encounter difficulties and experience this phase in a painful and tiring way. Therefore, it is advisable not to continue processing the trauma when the patient wants a break. In this regard, the patient has the possibility, when he wishes, to stop the processing, both during the sessions and between sessions, through the "stop" signals that he learned during Phase 2.

In this phase, the clinician must offer an environment of safety and protection but ensure that the patient is the active protagonist of the work on the trauma. The therapist can intervene when a blockage or excessive emotional load is created in the patient, activating the safe place or techniques for strengthening resources. It also has the role of encouraging the patient and taking care of maintaining the safe environment. In particular, to facilitate the processing of trauma, it can be helpful:

* Active coaching: the therapist must offer verbal support, useful to support and facilitate the processing of the trauma. Some sample comments, "Good! It's going well!"

* Working on external constraints: During the processing of trauma the patient may be distracted by external elements or circumstances that may interfere with the processing work (for example, the discovery of a family member's illness), so it is useful to manage them with the patient, rather than continuing to work actively on the trauma.

* Work in an experiential and co-participatory way: the clinician must be prepared to go where the patient's elaboration takes him/her. It is necessary for the therapist to remain in the real relationship in an authentic way (working alliance) and to be able to contain the traumas of the patient, keeping at bay his reactions against transferals, vicarious trauma and compassion fatigue.

In the final part of Phase 4, the clinician must ensure that the patient has actually released all of his pain and that the SOUTH scale has reached the score 0.

Even though the patient is in a position to get rid of the pain associated with the trauma, "he has not yet integrated a more adaptive perspective with which to look at what has happened".

➢ Phase 5: Installation

In this phase, the patient is asked for a positive cognition that can be the one selected in Phase 3 or another more appropriate one that emerged in Phase 4. This knowledge must be installed while the patient is performing eye movements. First it is installed by itself and then it is integrated with the souvenir-target. The objective is that the patient should feel it as his own and authentic, reporting a VOC score of 6 or 7. When the VOC scale score is not high, it may be a sign that some aspects of the memory have not been properly desensitized.

Before concluding Phase 5, the patient is congratulated for his work and for having overcome all those internal obstacles that prevented him from living in a harmonious and adaptive way. This phase, however, does not correspond to the end of the treatment, in fact, even if you have achieved a good result, you cannot yet be sure that the results obtained are permanent. It must be ensured that the effects of the treatment are maintained and have led the patient towards a healthier and more adaptive perspective.

➢ Phase 6: Body scanning

In addition to the work of remembering target and positive cognition, the patient is asked to check their body sensations and any tensions or discomforts in the body. Body scanning is an additional possibility to assess whether there is still some aspect of the unprocessed trauma. The body, in fact, is the repository of past traumas, and healing to be complete, requires that the body can also get rid of painful memories. When the patient feels painful sensations in the body, eye movements are performed.

In the EMDR treatment, awareness of body sensations is a key aspect in all eight phases. Specifically, however, the purpose of this phase is to go to the origin of the bodily sensations to bring out the traumas at even deeper levels, so that they can be completely reworked.

The body scanning phase can be said to be over when the patient is able to carry out a complete exploration of his body without finding any physical tension. If positive or comfortable sensations are reported, it is useful to strengthen them with some bilateral stimulation sets.

> ### Phase 7: Closure

Before concluding the session, it is important to help the patient develop a sense of self-control. It is also useful to leave him in a positive state, giving him the idea of having reached a goal, and prepare him to deal with possible effects of treatment during the interval between sessions, such as memories, feelings, images, disturbing thoughts. In this regard, patients are given the task of keeping a diary in which to record side effects between sessions, specifying that disorders that may emerge outside the session are part of the continuation of the healing process. It can also be useful to work on some structured questions that help the patient to give substance to what he has achieved and help him to be autonomous. Among the most frequently asked questions we can find:

- What was the most important part of the session for you?

- What was the part that put you most to the test?

- What did you learn from today's session?

- What strategies do you intend to put in place to keep up with the new things you've learned?

These instructions close the EMDR session, while treatment is not completed without step 8, i.e. re-evaluation.

> ### Phase 8: Revaluation

This phase takes place at the beginning of each session, following a previous session in which the EMDR was carried out, and consists of a re-evaluation of the previous treatment and its effects. It also provides the clinician with important information for determining the next course of action. It's useful in the revaluation:

* Ask the patient what he or she felt in the interval between sessions, to understand what has been processed and to understand what external events have occurred or may occur.

* Evaluate whether the improvements achieved during the therapy have been maintained during the week.

* Pay attention to the patient's criticism, especially if he feels stuck and thinks the processing is not working.

* Examine the diary to determine any objectives to be addressed.

* Re-evaluate positive cognition through the VOC scale.

Once the above issues have been resolved, the re-evaluation phase provides for a gradual reduction in the number of meetings.

The use of EMDR with children and adolescents

The standard EMDR protocol is modified when it is applied to children and adolescents, as working with individuals in their developmental age requires more attention. In particular, it is necessary to collaborate with parents throughout the therapeutic treatment, and develop and keep alive the motivation, as it is not the child who has asked to go to therapy. Moreover, children's attention times are shorter and there is still a difficulty in verbalization, so it is important to be more concrete and to give priority to the work on images, rather than on cognitions and emotions. Alternative techniques must also be used to induce eye movements, insert play elements, be flexible, resourceful and attentive to the needs of the child.

The most important thing when working with patients, especially children, is to ensure a constant sense of security. Following what he says, it is good to keep in mind a number of useful interventions to promote safety:

* The alliance with the parents: for the parents to show support for the treatment, the therapist must show respect and understanding for their values, their anxieties and concerns, avoiding arousing in them feelings of guilt. It may also be useful to assign them active roles within the treatment.

* The physical proximity of the parents: the children must know that the parents who accompany them are easily reachable. It can therefore be useful to keep the parent in the room and nearby, or to ensure that the child can be in the arms of the parent, especially if very young.

* Explanation of the procedure: For the child to understand EMDR, it is important to demonstrate to him that it is a safe technique. In this respect, it may be useful for a parent or family member to explain the procedure, or for the child and therapist to exchange roles and for the child to try to induce eye movements in the therapist.

* The relationship: to develop the collaboration of children it is useful to win them over by communicating warmth, showing sensitivity and concern, playing with them.

* The therapeutic relationship: it is something that goes beyond the simple relationship and that is built over time, thanks to the establishment of trust and positive results.

* Respect the child's time: there are some children who do not tolerate EMDR immediately, but need it to be introduced gradually, so it may be useful, for example, try the EMDR on a target with a low score SUD or use it first on a positive installation and then on the traumatic one.

* Positive installations: these installations allow the child to access the trauma in safer and more positive conditions. Among the most famous we have: "The safety device" that can be useful to introduce before facing a high score SOUTH and consists in helping the child to find those inner resources that allow him to deal with painful material. The most common security devices are: weapons, a helper, a parent, a guardian angel, a superhero or qualities, such as being bigger and stronger, "The safe place" which consists of asking the child to focus on a safe and desirable place, to view it, describe it or draw it. This image will then be installed, and it is important that the therapist guides the choice to prevent the image from being wasted and to ensure that it is unspoiled by elements that can make it unsafe. They are also useful "Resources or solutions" asking the patient to visualize, describe or draw the resources, the solution, the skills both fantastic and realistic, that allow to face and solve a problem.

* Stop" signals: it must be clear to the child that he or she can freely stop treatment when he or she wishes. To train him, it may be useful to have him practice with manual or verbal "stop" signals.

* Physical discomfort: with a child experiencing physical pain it is advisable to stop the treatment, with the adult, however, you would continue with the EMDR. Physical discomfort in children can be solved in other ways, for example by installing an image that eliminates the painful sensation.

EMDR for children and young people has a number of key components. Below we will present a series of elements, taken from the setting of the Shapiro, with some changes depending on the age of the patients. In particular, according to Greenwald, they are essential:

* The production of mental images: it is a technique always used with children and in a similar way to how it is used in adults. It consists in asking the child if in the selected memory there a particularly relevant aspect and that is seems to be the worst part. If the child experiences difficulties, the therapist can help him/her through the "menu technique", presenting a list of potentially appropriate choices to guide the patient in finding the right answer.

* Negative cognition: it can be a problematic moment with children and adolescents, as it can be difficult to arouse it. It is useful to continue, however, to proceed waiting for negative cognitions to occur spontaneously during eye movements with the image. Questions that may be appropriate to elicit the most appropriate answer may be: "When you now remember it, what do you say to yourself?", "What makes you believe in yourself?".

* Positive cognition: it can be useful to obtain it through creative activities such as drawing or other symbolic expressions.

* The cognition validity scale (COC): a variation with children can be the method "distance between hands", in which the therapist asks how much hurts the feeling you feel, and hands very far from each other indicate the worst feeling, hands semi-distant from each other indicate a rather bad feeling, hands very close to each other indicate a feeling unpleasant. Or you can use graphic scales in which the child is presented with a series of human faces with expressions ranging from sad to happy.

* Emotion: it is an aspect included in the process, except with very young children who are less than 5 years old. It consists of asking the child what kind of emotion accompanies the selected memory. If the child is unable to respond, images of faces that express emotions can be shown.

* The scale of subjective units of disturbance (SOUTH): with older children and adolescents the numerical format is used as in adults, for younger children it is useful to use alternative methods, such as "distance between hands". Another technique may be to ask the child to trace the sole of his foot on a large sheet of paper. When the child is asked to score SOUTH, he must draw a circle with a highlighter to indicate how unpleasant his feeling is. As the EMDR progresses, the rims to be very large, will have to become very small, until they are a dot inside the drawn foot.

*   Physical sensation: this element is used in the same way for children and adolescents as for adults, and the purpose is to investigate in which part of the body the subject feels the sensation.

* Eye movements: for adolescents and children, eye movements can be induced with the standard setting used with adults, but they have a shorter duration also because processing with children is very fast. With younger children, however, it is useful to use alternative means: "the special object" (you can use a magic wand, a puppet, a plastic sword or any other object, perhaps chosen by the child, that helps to keep it concentrated, to make the standard movements), "clap your hands lightly / with force" (the child claps his hand on each open hand of the therapist. He can also do this by using toys in the room), "sticking out fingers" (the therapist closes his hands and suddenly raises a finger of one hand and then the other. The child, observing the fingers coming out alternately, moves the eyes forward and backward), "the snap of the fingers" (both auditory and visual stimuli are used to help the child to keep focused on the movements), "the alternating movements" (there are children, especially children with ADHD or learning disabilities, who have difficulty following the standard movement, so it may be useful to follow other movements: circular, elliptical, diagonal, a crosswise 8), "points on the wall" (they can be used when the therapist's sight, during eye movements, can distract the child so he can choose points or objects on the wall at both ends of the child's field of vision, asking him to look at them alternately), "ball games" (during the conversation, perhaps on a traumatic memory, he can induce eye movements, throwing the ball, in turn, between child and therapist. When the therapist believes that it is the right time to induce eye movements, he asks the child to hit his knees alternately), "push" (it is the child who guides the movement by pushing the therapist's hand or an object), "color" (the movement is induced because the child is asked to color the page from one side to another, in this way follows his hand and the signs he traces), "the touch of the hand" (the child puts his hands on the therapist's knees and the therapist touches his hands alternately, asking the child to move his eyes), "other alternating stimuli" (alternating sounds, alternately hitting feet or knees, the beat), "options of a high technological level" (one of the best known is a stick with a luminous tip and a box containing a ray of light that moves from one side to the other).

The eight phases of EMDR in treatment for children and adolescents

The eight phases of EMDR according to Greenwald are described below. The approach is that of Shapiro (1995), with some modifications adapted to children.

> *First phase: the history of the patient and the treatment plan*

This first phase includes the initial contact and the history. With children it is useful to consider all those potentially problematic contexts, in particular family and school. It is also important to collaborate with the significant figures who take care of the child, in particular the parents. In addition to the standard evaluation, additional data is useful:

* It is important to trace a complete history to take into account all the factors, even the earlier ones, that may have had an influence on the current vulnerability;

* It is essential to obtain all the specific details of the problem, the environmental contingencies and the way in which the child describes it;

* It is useful to collect data regarding the details of the traumatic event, the child's strengths, abilities and preferences.

> *Second phase: preparation*

The EMDR and the benefits of the treatment are presented, and informed consent is obtained from the parents and the child. It is a useful moment to know the difficulties and the potentialities of the patient, to understand what it is necessary to work on in order for the treatment to be successful. The important elements to be taken into account are:

* be aware of possible physiological, psychotic, dissociative problems, medication, violence. An important element to be addressed is when the child is followed up in the investigative and judicial spheres. In fact, the validity of memories could be compromised, so it is useful to evaluate the effects that EMDR could have on the memory of the child, on his will and on the ability to testify;

* have patience and understanding in the face of children's lack of motivation and parents' concerns. Motivation develops as the child understands the benefits of treatment, so it is important to set goals, have family support, create fun and engaging situations;

* use metaphors to explain how EMDR works and what the potential benefits of treatment are. The most common metaphors are the "rapid eye movements in dreams" (explaining to the child that while dreaming the eyes move very fast back and forth, and that for this reason dreaming makes you feel better when you wake up. Then make it clear that eye movements with EMDR are a similar process), the "video recorder" (explain to the child that what you will do, the recall of memories and scenes, will be like watching a movie on the video recorder), the "chest of drawers" (make the patient imagine a chest of drawers, to find out what is inside), the "laser gun" (to help the child to make unpleasant things disappear), the "dislocated finger" (explain to the child that as with a dislocation the feelings suffered make him feel very sick, and that to get better you have to wait to heal);

* use stuffed animals as they can function as alter egos, and be useful for working on symptoms, feelings and evaluations. More concretely, they can be used to illustrate the functioning of the EMDR to the child, to encourage him to participate, and to induce eye movements by holding the animal in the child's arms;

*   Presenting the EMDR in the form of a game can be useful to encourage the child's collaboration. For example, the plush animal can be used, the drawing of the outline of the foot, the training "Stop means stop".

> *Phase three: assessment*

This stage includes the evaluation of the souvenir-target in particular:

* Target identification: for the choice of a target, the mental image is used, which allows both to recover memories and to work on the installations, and also promotes concentration and commitment. In particular, with children, it is useful to refer to nightmares, being a common time for children with disorders. The choice of goal can emerge from the history of trauma, conversation, therapy or play. Once the objective has been chosen, work is carried out with EMDR.

* The SOUTH and VOC scales: allow to verify the processing, provide the patient with a way to evaluate progress, self-awareness and self-control. With children, most therapists use the SOUTH scale and not the VOC scale, but when EMDR's work focuses on cognitive aspects, for example with children who are victims of violence, it is advisable not to use the SOUTH scale.

> *Phase four: desensitization*

As in adults, eye movements are stimulated, while the patient focuses on the souvenir-target. Gradually the patient overcomes the various aspects of memory, including emotions, image, cognition and negative sensations. Working with children, however, requires changes, especially with very small children who often fail to bring out useful material during eye movements. It is advisable, therefore, not to fill them with questions to get an answer and continue to work on the goal until you reset the score SOUTH. At this stage, attention must be paid to certain elements:

* the impasses that appear when the child loses his or her motivation or fails to tolerate the level of suffering, so he or she can refuse to cooperate, producing no movement. These problems must be identified early and resolved. First you have to make sure that the child understands the procedure, then you have to check that the procedure is suitable for the child, and finally help the child find the right motivation to continue;

* between sessions, which can be managed by teaching the child breathing techniques. With children it is not only a relaxation technique, but also an element of playfulness that helps to keep them motivated;

* When achieving a zero SOUTH score, other objectives must be found to improve the effect of the treatment. To find them it is possible to make use of "cleaning up" (asking a series of questions concerning elements of problematic memory) and "developing the theme" (also working with elements related to disturbing memory, which may seem less relevant than the main objectives).

> *Fifth phase: installation*

Images are also used for installation. These installations allow the child to deal with the disturbing images before they are reworked. They can also be used when the SOUTH score does not drop or when the session is blocked. Among the most important installations we have:

* The safe place: the child is asked to choose a special place, to observe and describe it in detail and to notice how safe and protected he feels. It is installed by having the child focus on this image while making eye movements. It can be useful as a relaxation before EMDR, before desensitization, in the closing phase.

* The safety device: it is an installation useful to face a fantastic element like the nightmare. It is very useful when the child is afraid, when the processing has run aground, or in anxious disorders.

* The resolving image: a drawing is installed in which a problem is represented for the child and an attempt is made to solve it by asking the child to think of something alternative to the disturbing image.

* The fantastic solution: to suggest to the child to imagine making the painful element explode or disappear. It will introduce, thus, an aspect of play and fun, and the perception of having control.

* Past successes and positive feelings: after processing a painful memory, you can install an image linked to positive experiences and success.

* Future successes and positive feelings: the installation of a success in a field that constitutes the goal of the treatment.

* Extend safety: install a safety knowledge both on the target image and on all those places where the child has shown fear.

* The role/ideal model of the ego: when the child cannot tell a story of success and positive feelings, someone else's story is installed.

* The helper: father, mother, guardian angel, the role model or the current self of the child.

* Skills and knowledge: install skills or study content to improve learning skills.

* Correction of negative aspects: a negative cognition can be modified by installing a correction found by the patient.

* The inner goodness: in front of those children who are convinced to be bad, you can install the feeling of being a good person.

* Cognitive Restructuring: Replacing negative cognitions by installing positive and more adaptive cognitions.

* The container: to make people imagine, visualize and install a container in which they conserve capacities and resources that can be used later on, training the child in how to access them.

> *Sixth phase: body scanning*

Ask the child, as for adults, to listen to their own body and notice if there are physical sensations of discomfort, and then work on it through eye movements.

> *Seventh phase: closure*

The child must be helped to acquire control and mastery before leaving the session. Three elements are important:

* Consolidation: it is useful to consolidate some of the results achieved in the session (for example, if the child has gained confidence and processed the fear, you can ask him to demonstrate his courage by making him fight puppets).

* The container: install an image, such as a box, to contain everything that is annoying or has not yet been resolved.

* Closure: positive installations, relaxation exercises, rituals (how to put away games).

> *Phase 8: revaluation*

After EMDR, it is useful to carry out an evaluation of the effects and results of the treatment, and to establish the lines of action for the next session. In addition, it is useful to ask the child to show what they have acquired through play or other behavior.

Special applications

This section presents some particular situations in which EMDR must be applied with particular regard to and adaptation to the subjects and the situations taken into account. Following the setting of, the EMDR undergoes changes with:

* Infants and young children in their first steps: when treating very young children, the EMDR procedure is shorter and the presence of parents is very important, as they become part of the treatment. Most newborns and first-time children are treated for problems caused by trauma, such as a car accident or abuse. These issues, which also affect parents, can also be addressed in a single session. It is important to take into account the reaction of the parents. In fact, in front of their suffering child, parents show different feelings: sadness, anger, sense of responsibility, post-traumatic reactions, even violent. All these reactions affect the way the child is cared for, so individual treatment may be necessary. It is also effective to make parents active in the treatment of the child to regain their sense of effectiveness. If a parent feels more efficient, the child will also receive better care. It is necessary to take care of the cultural preparation of the parents, often, in fact, the parents, in front of a traumatized child, do not know how to behave towards him. The therapist's task is to evaluate each individual situation in order to be able to give the most suitable advice to the parents. The involvement of the parents in the treatment is fundamental, so that the therapy can be concluded with positive results. It is useful for the parent to be present during the treatment, to hold the child in his arms and to participate with the therapist in the EMDR, for example by saying key words related to the trauma with him or by drumming on his feet.

*   Families: it is essential to encourage parents to help their child in the treatment of EMDR. The collaboration and support of the parents is useful for the realization of an individual treatment with the child. Some theorists believe that parents should be specifically informed about EMDR, while others believe that parents should be informed only in general. The choice also depends on the cultural level of the parents and how much they want to be informed. It is essential, however, to stay in touch with the parents, because they are valuable informants to understand the progress of the child, his behavior, symptoms, the way in which they relate to him and to be aware of what happens between sessions. The role of parents is fundamental to treatment for several reasons:

- bringing the child to therapy is a sign of trust, cooperation and approval towards the therapist who must, throughout the treatment, develop and maintain a therapeutic alliance with them;

- Parents provide essential information for the initial assessment, to know the progress, to choose the objectives and the installations. In particular, they provide information about the history of trauma, the child's behavior, interests, abilities and weaknesses;

- The parent can be the first to try the EMDR and show the child that they can trust and feel protected;

- For many children, especially the frightened ones, it is important to have the parent there with them in the seat or nearby;

- It is important that parents communicate with the therapist between sessions to inform the therapist of the reactions of the child after each session;

- Parents often ask for treatment, and in this case, desensitization can help them to respond in a more adaptive way, but most of the time, working with parents, consists of making them aware of their child's difficulties and behaving more consistently towards them.

Some corrective measures to be taken by parents with regard to their children may be useful:

- "appealing to the rules": the rules and authority of adults are fundamental for children, as they increase their self-confidence. The rules are installed first in the memory of the parent, then in that of the child and finally mental images of difficult situations will be installed in which the rules chosen previously are applied;

- "What a good child": this intervention is carried out when the child feels "bad", and the corrective intervention is transmitted by the parents, as they represent the main authoritative source. This intervention also has positive effects on parents who discover the goodness of the child and learn to distinguish positive and negative feelings and reactions towards him.

- "The child's story": When faced with a traumatized child, parents often also present secondary traumas, such as guilt and vulnerability. This condition could have consequences for the child's chances of recovery. So, you can ask the parent to write the story of your child in the form of a fairy tale. The protagonist must have the same characteristics as the child, the language used must be simple and understandable to the child and the story must present a positive beginning of life, then a part dedicated to the traumatic experience, with the characteristics of the child's trauma and finally the resolution of the situation. This story is modified and adapted by the therapist, if necessary, and then used in the EMDR session, associated with eye movements.

* Wetting the bed: enuresis is a very common problem among children who have suffered trauma and is one of the central objectives in the treatment. Some interventions are presented to eliminate this symptom:

- evaluate all possible factors that triggered enuresis and ensure that there are no biological causes;

- enuresis is often a post-traumatic symptom, which disappears with the processing of trauma, so you can use EMDR on traumatic memories, nightmares and night fears;

- making use of the positive parental function is an important part of the treatment in which parents must create a protected and corrective environment for the child;

- to develop the habit of continence, establishing regular timetables for the intake of meals and drinks;

- The treatment should help the child to become stronger, and the therapist appeals to the fact that strength is also synonymous with maturity, so you can ask the child to practice proving to be strong, for example with physical exercise or you can install role models with figures with which the child identifies and does not wet the bed;

- teach the child exercises to develop muscles related to continence and urination;

- to make the problem personified, as if it were something external, to describe and draw it and then to elaborate it with the EMDR;

- create successful experiences and encourage them through positive rewards and reinforcements.

* Treatment situations: This section covers a number of special situations, including:

- the treatment of outpatients: with children who are not too severe, EMDR can also start from the second session. The first interview is used to get the necessary information from the parents, create an alliance with them. A separate interview explains the treatment to the child, tries to develop the motivation and identifies the objectives. The first session deals with the evaluation and involvement of parents and the child. The following sessions, instead, will always begin with a control with the parents on the progress of the child and a control with the child through drawings and play, then move on to the EMDR and finally to the activity of play useful to consolidate the results obtained.

- The extraordinary treatment: these are usually patients sent by other therapists, so it is important to make an initial assessment with the child, parents and the principal therapist. The EMDR therapist will act as a consultant, while the main therapist will always be responsible for the case.

- Environmental therapy: in this type of treatment the objective is to intervene on negative behavior, and EMDR is carried out only when a safe and more favorable context for recovery has been created.

- Schools: The first step for the therapist is to enter the school and be accepted as a member, alongside parents and teachers. It is also necessary to plan with the teachers when and for how long the child can be removed from school activities to go to therapy. In this case, EMDR can be useful for working on trauma, coping skills, study skills, school exercises and school frustrations.

- Children in hospital: In this context, EMDR is only used at a later stage. The first objective is to help parents cope with the situation. EMDR can be used to install visualizations related to the inner healing process, to elaborate a modification in the image itself, to prepare the child to accept medical treatments, to elaborate a trauma, including hospitalization itself.

- Disasters, accidents and other critical situations: in these circumstances it may be useful to treat children with EMDR and work with the family to reduce stress levels. Work is done on post-traumatic symptoms, but clinicians must be prepared to work on previous traumas and leaks as well.

* Particular populations, among these we find:

- "ADHD and Learning Disorders": According to Dunton, with these types of disorders it is appropriate to apply a step-by-step approach, to focus on positive installations directed towards self-esteem, social and learning capacities and school skills. With these children it is often useful to activate eye movements with alternative methods such as hand strokes, finger snaps, the method of "points on the wall". Often these children have a long experience of trauma, but it is worthwhile to start working on more recent episodes.

- "Children who are victims of violence": the first step is to ensure that the child has control over the situation and can experience security. EMDR is useful for processing what happened, starting with the most recent and worst memories. It is also useful to understand if children suffer from dissociative disorders.

- "Reactive attachment disorder": When using EMDR on the trauma of these patients, the focus is mainly on anger, the transition from the knowledge of feeling bad to a more positive one, or it can help to develop attachment to parents.

- "Obsessive-compulsive disorder": for some scholars, people suffering from this disorder, due to particular neurological characteristics, would be incompatible with this type of treatment, but the results show the opposite.

- "Tourette-like disorder": for these patients, EMDR can be useful to move a tick from a visible and perhaps embarrassing area of the body to an alternative that is less noticeable. In addition, tics are generated by stress, so you can also work on sources of stress and relaxation.

- "Somatic disorders": for these cases it is useful to teach techniques of pain control, then work on stress and psychological suffering.

- "Physical pain": the first step is to work on pain, which sometimes seems to be a container for psychological pain, then it is useful to find the traumatic source of pain (accidents, violence, discovery of a disease...) and process it with the EMDR or, if there is no memory related to pain, you can work with the EMDR directly on pain. There may be cases of patients with permanent damage, so it may be useful to help them adapt to the damage they have suffered, working on both trauma and fear of the future, using EMDR.

Research: a course on the main studies

The studies on EMDR collected in recent years have demonstrated the effectiveness of the method, especially for the treatment of PTSD in very different traumatic situations: wars, accidents, burns, current or past sexual violence, natural disasters, bereavement, terrorist acts.

The first controlled study (Shapiro, 1989) succeeded in demonstrating the effectiveness of this technique and the reduction of anxiety on 22 subjects who had suffered traumas of various kinds. Significant results were already demonstrated at the first session and were maintained at follow-up three months later for the group of subjects to whom the EMDR had been administered. The control group, on the other hand, which had been given a modified treatment, did not demonstrate a decrease in SOUTH levels after the session. Subsequent cline data began to encourage the effectiveness of this technique. In this respect, we recall the clinical case of Wolpe and Abrams of a 43-year-old woman, who was diagnosed with PTSD after a rape that occurred 10 years before and who demonstrated successful improvements following EMDR treatment, in contrast to previous behavioral therapy with lower change results. Also important are the two clinical cases followed by Puk, victims of sexual abuse in childhood. In particular, one woman continued to suffer from nightmares and an inability to relate to men. After 3 sets of eye movements, the SOUTH scale went down to zero and the nightmares decreased significantly. At a 12-month follow-up, the woman had only one nightmare and one sexual relationship with a man. Kleinknecht and Morgan reported the case of a 40-year-old man with PTSD, following an accident in which he was injured. After the treatment, the patient improved and showed no more symptoms. In addition, the results were maintained at a follow-up of 8 months.

Following these important results, many controlled studies were carried out to demonstrate the efficacy of EMDR in the treatment of PTSD, including Rothbaum, who conducted a study on a sample of 21 women who had been raped. These women were treated with 90-minute EMDR sessions and compared with a control group. After 3 sessions, most women no longer met the criteria for PTSD, unlike the control group, which showed little improvement. In addition, the results were maintained at a follow-up of 3 months. Marcus, Marquis and Sakai worked on a sample of 67 subjects with PTSD, treated with 3 sessions of 90-minute EMDR. The results showed that all victims of a single trauma and 70% of those with the most trauma no longer met the PTSD criteria. Wilson, Becker and Tinker, out of a sample of 80 adults with traumatic experiences, 36 of whom were diagnosed with PTSD, demonstrated the efficacy of EMDR at a follow-up of 15 months, with a decrease of 68% in PTSD symptoms and 84% in the diagnosis of PTSD. In a study by Marcus, Steven, Marquis, Priscilla, Sakai, Caroline, the 67 patients examined underwent EMDR treatment for the treatment of PTSD. The study showed that a relatively small number of EMDR treatment sessions can bring substantial benefits that are maintained over time.

EMDR has also been very successful in treating PTSD with veterans and war veterans, so much so that the Veterans Health Affaire National Clinical Practice Guideline Council and the U.S. Department of Defense have included EMDR in their special programs for PTSD in military and non-military populations, along with cognitive psychotherapy, exposure and Stress Inoculation Training. In this regard, a study by Carlson, Chemtob, Rusnak, Hedlund, Muraoka showed that after 12 sessions of EMDR, 78% of war veterans, were no longer covered by the diagnosis of PTSD. A German study of 80 German soldiers admitted between 1998 and 2002, diagnosed with PTSD, also showed significant improvements immediately after treatment with EMDR, keeping them at a follow-up of 29 months.

Numerous studies have also demonstrated the effectiveness of EMDR in the treatment of PTSD in children. In a study by Ahmad, Larsson, Sundelin-Wahlsten, the aim was to examine the efficacy of EMDR treatment for children with post-traumatic stress disorder compared to a group of children not treated with EMDR. The sample taken into consideration included 33 subjects, selected from a waiting list in a psychiatric clinic. These were children diagnosed with PTSD, at least 6 years old, who had experienced trauma at least once or had grown up in traumatic environments (sexual abuse, road accidents, bereavement...). The duration between the traumatic event and the diagnosis of PTSD was less than a year. The 33 children who had met the criteria were subjected to EMDR treatment and a pre-treatment evaluation programmed immediately after the randomization trial and post-treatment 2 months later. The children in the treatment group had received EMDR immediately after the pre-treatment trial, while the others had to wait 2 months before receiving the same treatment. The EMDR treatment used was inspired by the standard protocol with some adaptations for children. Despite the limited sample size, children treated with EMDR showed a significant improvement in PTSD symptoms, unlike untreated children.

A study by Aduriz, Bluthgen and Knopfler operated on 124 children (4 to 17 years old) who had suffered trauma following a severe flood that hit Santa Fe on 30 April 2003. The intervention involved one treatment through EMDR after the disaster and another after 3 months to evaluate the results. The results demonstrated a statistically significant reduction in symptoms immediately after surgery. These statistically significant differences were maintained even after three months, as measured by the psychometric scales and by clinical and behavioral observation. Despite methodological limitations, this study supports the effectiveness of EMDR therapy in the improvement and prevention of PTSD, offering an efficient, simple and economical tool. EMDR was also successfully used on children in group contexts, particularly in Mexico, Venezuela, El Salvador, with Albanian children in a refugee camp in Germany. The effectiveness of EMDR has also been demonstrated by comparing it with other types of interventions. An interesting study was concerned with demonstrating the greater efficiency of EMDR compared to other therapies, in particular exposure therapy and relaxation therapies. The results showed a greater reduction in PTSD symptoms, particularly with regard to intrusive symptoms, such as flashbacks and nightmares, in subjects treated with EMDR. Silver, Brooks and Obenchain's study of a group of veterans with PTSD also showed that subjects treated with relaxation techniques and EMDR showed more improvement than those treated only with relaxation techniques. Another study by Scheck et al. on a sample of 60 women victims of rape, who underwent two EMDR or active listening sessions. Although the treatment was short-lived, EMDR proved more effective than active listening. In a meta-analysis study conducted by Van Etten and Taylor (1998) which covered the results of 59 treatments in 32 studies involving patients with PTSD, and which considered different therapies, including: pharmacotherapy, behavioral therapy, EMDR, relaxation therapy, hydrotherapy, hypnotherapy, emphasized that EMDR and behavioral therapy proved to be the most effective therapies, with the difference that EMDR was shorter in meeting improvements in the diagnosis of PTSD and the effects tended to increase in subsequent follow-up. Lee, Gavriel, Drummond, Richards and Greenwald, on a sample of 22 subjects, who underwent 7 therapeutic sessions, compared EMDR with stress inoculation therapy and prolonged exposure. EMDR proved to be more effective in treating symptoms of intrusiveness, and in maintaining the results at a later follow-up. In a study by Ironson, Freund, Strauss and Williams, which involved a sample of 22 patients, he demonstrated that after 3 sessions of EMDR the symptoms of PTSD and depression decreased significantly. In addition, the effects were maintained at a follow-up of 3 months and treatment proved faster with EMDR, rather than with behavioral therapy.

In the last twenty years, EMDR has been the subject of central study in scientific research in the field of traumatic stress therapy, proving to be an effective tool. This procedure continues to arouse great interest and curiosity, and the studies aimed at improving it are still in progress, especially with regard to the understanding of the neurobiological foundations underlying the treatment, still little-known today.

CHAPTER TWO:
PSYCHIC TRAUMA

"When you live a truly unpleasant experience, there are two things you can do, two are the ways you can go. One is to look in the face the memory of that experience, continue to think about it, talk about it and feel about it: it can be difficult, but it is as if every time you give that memory a little bite, chew it well and digest it. It then becomes part of our nourishment and helps us to grow. And the part that hurts gets smaller and smaller. When you say that through difficult times you become stronger, and that's what you refer to. Unfortunately, sometimes people go the other way. The memory is so painful, it hurts so much that you just want to drive it away, you want to put a wall between us and him, you just want to feel good and be able to keep the day going. This works, at least for a while; it gives us relief. But the problem is that the memory does not go away, it is always there, fresh as the day the event happened, always ready to reappear to be chewed completely and digested so as to become part of the past. And then, every time, there's something that makes us think about that memory again, as if it said, 'Hey, I'm here too, can you let me in now?'. Here's an example, almost all of us, if walking we are accidentally bumped by someone, well, maybe we dry up a bit for a few seconds, but no more, just one: 'Sorry', and it all ends. But if the person who is hit has a lot of compressed anger behind that wall, he will have the same normal minimum reaction as us, with all the material behind the wall that says, 'I do too,' so that the person will be so out of his pants that he's ready to fight. This is the problem: the material behind the wall; it can jump on us at any time and provoke excessive reactions in us, making things easy. So sometimes people, when they get sick because of these problems, go to a therapist to get help. And with his help he manages to grasp what he has chased behind the wall: he takes a piece of that memory, chews it well, digests it and becomes much stronger. With the EMDR something very similar happens to what happens with other therapies: you can pick up what's behind the wall, you take a piece of it, you chew it well, that's all. Only that with the EMDR you can relive the various pieces of the bad memory much faster, maybe you go over an entire memory in just two sessions, sometimes more, sometimes less".

Greenwald, 2000

EMDR, Eye Movement Desensitization and Reprocessing, is an innovative psychotherapeutic tool, born just over twenty years ago, thanks to the discovery of Francine Shapiro. It is used, in particular, for the treatment of PTSD and traumatic memories. EMDR seems to have proven its effectiveness even with traumatized children and adolescents, proving to be even faster.

The standard EMDR procedure consists of eight phases that include "non-specific" elements concerning the patient-therapist relationship, "specific" elements, i.e. eye movements or other stimulations, and elements derived from other clinical traditions, such as resource installations, visualizations, use of images, cognitive assessment.

The fundamental characteristic is that, within a global psychotherapeutic plan, through bilateral stimulation work, while the patient focuses on the disturbing part of traumatic memory, it is possible to obtain, quickly and effectively, the desensitization and re-elaboration of traumatic memories. The desensitization and reworking of every aspect of traumatic memory and related memories allows to integrate traumatic memories, to create more adaptive associations and to give rise to a cognitive and emotional restructuring.

From a theoretical point of view, the EMDR starts from the assumption that this procedure has the ability to activate a neuropsychologically innate mechanism, typical of each person, which is that of information processing, or "some types of stimulations produced by the therapist within a dual field of attention, with the attention paid simultaneously on the one hand to an external stimulus produced by the therapist, on the other hand to the flow of mental processing, activate an effective process of accelerated and ecological processing of information. It is therefore assumed that the patient possesses the resources necessary for the emotional and cognitive processing of a traumatic memory, and that the therapist has the role of facilitating this process. The discovery of Francine Shapiro in 1987 challenged traditional clinical treatments for the treatment of trauma, and after just over twenty years continues to amaze, to be the subject of treatment and research and to demonstrate its success and effectiveness. In fact, originally, EMDR was rejected by the scientific community, but the studies, 16 of which were randomized, managed to demonstrate its effectiveness. Today, EMDR has established itself as the most effective treatment for PTSD, succeeding in demonstrating its effectiveness not only in resolving traumatic memories, but also in producing global and more adaptive changes. In addition, many therapists use EMDR not only for the treatment of PTSD, but also for other clinical disorders, such as anxiety disorders, somatization disorders, dissociative disorders, eating disorders, mood disorders, sexual disorders. The use of EMDR for all clinical disorders, with the exception of PTSD, is currently considered the most experimental part and research and clinical studies are still ongoing. Although EMDR has been a great success in 20 years, it still has a long way to go.

The work of this thesis aims at presenting and deepening this innovative procedure, through a theoretical clarification, a collection and a reflection of the most important research on EMDR and its applications in the clinical field.

The first chapter is dedicated to a deepening of psychic trauma. In particular, this concept is defined, with a reflection that starts from the definition given by the DSM-IV-TR and then extends to concepts such as "complex trauma" and "early relational trauma". It then presents the most important historical origins and theoretical contributions that have expanded the concept of trauma, with particular attention to the role that psychoanalysis has played. A wide reflection is dedicated to the contribution of attachment theory and its developments in the cognitivist field, in which, in particular Liotti, has deepened the concept of "fear without an outlet", characteristic of disorganized attachment. Finally, the diagnostic category of "Post-traumatic Stress Disorder" according to the DSM-IV-TR is presented, as well as the "Post-traumatic Complex Stress Disorder", formulated for the first time by Judith Herman (1992) to overcome the limits and incompleteness of the diagnostic category of PTSD. The chapter concludes with a description of further disorders caused by traumatic experiences.

The second chapter is dedicated to Eye Movement Desensitization and Reprocessing (EMDR), with a definition of the procedure and a description of its origins and uses in the clinical setting. The theoretical bases on which EMDR is based are then presented with an in-depth analysis of the AIP (Adaptive Information Processing) model. In addition, the standard EMDR protocol is presented in detail, with an explanation of the characteristic instruments and the eight phases of the procedure, and the use of EMDR with children and adolescents is described, highlighting the changes and adaptations applied for these age groups. The chapter concludes with a collection of the main researches that have allowed to demonstrate the effectiveness of EMDR in the treatment of PTSD.

The third chapter is an in-depth study of Anxiety Disorders, with a reflection of the theories on anxiety, the classification of Anxiety Disorders according to the DSM-IV-TR and a description of the generative processes of maintenance and the psychopathological beliefs underlying these disorders. It is then presented a deepening of the Anxiety Disorders in the evolutionary age.

The fourth chapter is an attempt to demonstrate the applicability of EMDR to other clinical conditions beyond PTSD, in particular Anxiety Disorders. Although research into clinical disorders other than PTSD is still scarce and with many limitations, it has been possible to collect all the studies carried out for each of the Anxiety Disorders and it has been possible to make a reflection on the effectiveness or otherwise of EMDR. The last part of the chapter includes an example description of the EMDR procedure on Panic Disorder.

The thesis also includes an appendix in which are reported some clinical examples that have as their object the EMDR treatment of some children. In particular, the work concerned the transcription of the sessions and the choice of some significant parts of it to provide a practical illustration of the EMDR procedure.

Psychic trauma

In the DSM-IV-TR (American Psychiatric Association, 2000), the only disorder that involves trauma as an etiological agent, is Post-Traumatic Stress Disorder (PTSD). Here trauma is defined as a factor in which the subject lives, assists or encounters one or more events that may involve death, serious injury or a threat to the physical integrity of both himself and others. Among the traumatic events we can find torture, physical or sexual abuse, assaults, accidents, serious illnesses, natural disasters, etc. The definition given by the DSM-IV-TR (American Psychiatric Association, 2000) is, however, restrictive, as it favors an objective evaluation of trauma and tends to take into account common events, concrete and easily placed in time and space. It concerns psychopathological reactions that are valid for a single traumatic event, or for a limited number of traumas, and therefore it is not suitable for the description of complex, cumulative traumas that occurred in distant periods, particularly in childhood. Trauma, in fact, is a much broader concept that can compromise the sense of self integrity. In particular, trauma can concern experiences of environmental and interpersonal failure, such as separation, neglect, psychological violence, which have consequences on the emotional, cognitive, emotional, emotional and relational functioning of the child. "Diagnosis of PTSD is not enough to capture the complexity of trauma-related suffering."

Wanting to give a definition of "complex trauma", which refers to multiple traumatic events, chronic, prolonged, interpersonal in nature, often in the primary care system, early onset, it covers all "those conditions continuous or temporary, cumulative or sudden that lead to deprivation by excess or defect on the body and mind growing". "As a result of these early deprivations and the unavailability of caregivers, there is an overwhelming of the self in training, which is forced to suffer a situation of helplessness and anguish. According to Borgo no, these subjects live experiences of psychic annihilation, with the consequent loss of authentic subjectivity and of autonomous and different psychic existence. What makes the trauma traumatic is not so much the events in themselves that are repeated cumulatively, but the fact that the subject is not assisted, remains alone and suffers a "hit-and-run omission". Trauma does not find an environment capable of welcoming it, containing it and recognizing it. The terrifying and incomprehensible experience is denied, ignored, not integrated, so it is not psychically representable. As a result, your psyche is deprived of its own mental spaces. "The child is in fact expropriated of something of his own and of specific, finding himself deposited internally something alien and foreign, which comes from others and that in many cases kills every life and every growth. Complex trauma, therefore, can have significantly serious effects, especially when the person who suffers it is in the full development of his or her personality. It undermines all those "capacities of psychobiological self-regulation, of adaptation to the interpersonal environment, of constructing the image of oneself [...] in the regulation of emotions" and can lead to the appearance of symptoms of PTSD, of dissociation and alteration of identity.

In conclusion, we can draw attention to the fact that trauma can be conceived in different ways: as a "traumatic event", a single, circumscribed stressful event that threatens the subject's ability to resist, as a "traumatic development", traumas that are repeated cumulatively, from which it is impossible to escape. It is, therefore, a question of complex traumas. Recently we have started to talk about another type of trauma, the "early relational trauma", a type of complex trauma, characteristic of the first two years of life, which coincides with the disorganization of attachment, characterized by interactions between the child and the caregiver based on a contagion of fear, expressed by the adult and absorbed by the child. This type of fear is called "fear without an outlet", and is determined by caregiver figures neglecting, mistreating, disassociated, frightened, which presence does not provide protection and security, but danger and repeated trauma. In the face of this terror, the child has no way out, no solution and, as a consequence, no possibility to organize and integrate his attachment system in an adaptive and coherent way. "If interpersonal threat conditions occur repeatedly during childhood and adolescence (or do not combine with particular protective factors), they lead to traumatic development and can cause dissociative dimension disorders and a wide psychopathological and physical vulnerability.

The historical origins of psychic trauma

The concept of trauma was born around 1880 in the neurological field. In 1883 Herbert Page published an article on railway accidents and formulated the concept of "nervous shock", identifying fear as the cause of nervous symptoms. In 1884 Adolf Strumpell, deepening his studies of Page, built the notion of "psychic trauma".

The most important contribution in those years was made by Jean Martin Charcot (1890) with his notion of "hysterical-traumatic paralysis". According to Charcot, a psychic shock generates the idea of serious damage that can turn into a pathogenic idea and produce symptoms, in particular paralysis. This theory was a decisive moment of change, as the idea of having to interpret psychologically the post-traumatic symptoms spread. But, above all, thanks to Charcot, the concept of hysteria began to be understood from a psychological point of view and interpreted starting from the trauma. In 1889 Pierre Janet hypothesized that the hysterical-traumatic symptoms were caused by an inability of the subject to remove the emotions and memories related to the trauma. According to Janet, traumatic memories remained dissociated and fixed in an unconscious part of the mind and were not coherently and adaptively integrated into psychic activities. The neurologist Hermann Oppenheim, who formulated the diagnostic category of "traumatic neurosis" in 1888, also had the same idea.

With the First World War, this theme was abandoned, despite the fact that traumatic neurosis and post-traumatic symptoms were common. The notion of traumatic neurosis began to be considered again by the scientific community after the Vietnam War. In 1980, in fact, the diagnostic category of "Post-Traumatic Stress Disorder" (PTSD) was introduced in the DSM-III (American Psychiatric Association, 1980). The new diagnostic category again focused attention on psychic trauma, and studies, in addition to being interested in the problems posed by war veterans, expanded to other topics such as the Holocaust and physical and sexual abuse in childhood, until the birth of a new discipline, the "psych traumatology".

Among the origins of psychic trauma, it is fundamental to recognize the role of psychoanalysis, which, unlike the descriptive/classificatory approach, tried to broaden the concept, going to understand the origin, the quality, the way of acting and the consequences of trauma. It was Freud who treated the adult symptoms, at the time considered signs of a neuropathic predisposition, and considered a "childhood trauma" at the origin of these symptoms. Initially he embraced Charcot's studies (1890) on hysterical-traumatic paralysis. But the decisive step was the "cathartic model", at the basis of which the traumatic disorder is the consequence of the removal and therefore of the traumatic episode that is not sufficiently discharged. With the cathartic method Freud (1892-1895) tried to recall, in his patients, the traumatic experience, to allow the discharge. This way of proceeding led Freud to notice that at the base of the traumas were childish situations of seduction or sexual abuse. In 1896 he formulated the "theory of seduction", claiming that at the basis of the neurotic symptom were experiences of early sexual abuse, and began to consider childhood trauma as a direct cause of psychoneurosis. Shortly afterwards, however, in 1897, he changed the theory, abandoned the idea of childhood trauma as a real event and began to consider it, instead, as a phantasmagorical construction. For Freud, hysterical symptoms became the symbolic expression of the conflict between unconscious desires and ego defenses.

After twenty years of neglect, the theory of trauma re-emerged and was re-evaluated, thanks to the contribution of Sandor Ferenczi. His interest in trauma was reawakened when he was appointed a military physician in World War I. In this period Ferenczi (1916, 1919) formulated the notion of "narcissistic wound", according to which, the typical regression of war neurosis, was linked to a wound of the ego, of self-love. Later Ferenczi tried to treat the trauma by referring also to Freud's biological studies, claiming that the body can be used to externalize unconscious fantasies. "Thus, the idea of trauma is rediscovered in the original meaning of wound on the living body, because it is a wound that not only affects an anatomical part, but also the meaning that this part has for the subject: a mutilation of the face, for example, hurts the sense that the ego has of itself in relation to others. In short, the body is at the center of a way of meaning and it is this world that is upset by the trauma". So, if for Freud trauma generates a pathogenic idea and therefore a new meaning, in Ferenczi, instead, it is something that disintegrates and fragments the mind into several parts. More precisely, according to Ferenczi (1929), trauma is "a subtraction of something that modifies the natural initiation to psychic life through operations of intrusion and extraction that mark and damage the experience of the child", "an interpersonal event that induces a coercive block in the evolutionary potential of the child towards birth and life".

According to Ferenczi (1931), the individual develops, grows and can give rise to his own Self thanks to an environment that knows how to contain, give shape, meanings and appropriate care. However, when the environment proves to be inadequate and confronts it with traumatic situations, the child feels a strong sense of anguish. The most significant aspect, however, that contributes to making the trauma "traumatic" is the mechanism of "denial" put in place by the adult who denies and disowns the reality of the child. This diversion and non-recognition, paralyzes thought, deprives the mind of its own mental spaces and threatens the subjectivity of the child. For a child, being able to overcome fear and pain, it is essential to share, listen to and support the parent. When this does not happen, the child remains alone in his despair: "The adult, who almost always acts as if nothing had happened, forbids the child not only to use the word, but also the possibility of creating a representation and a fantasy. The child's words remain buried alive and, because of this, under the pressure of other traumatic events, a fragmentation of the personality can be produced". Faced with this "no way out" situation. "The only possibility of salvation is an autoplastic restructuring of the personality: a part of the psychic structure (the one that is suffering and feels the deadly danger in action) is separated and removed from the source of danger, is hidden in the depths of the unconscious, a place apparently safe and sheltered from what is happening [...] peace is achieved with self-destruction with self-mutilation or parts of oneself.

As a consequence, the traumatic event does not have the possibility of being inscribed and placed in the psyche, thus becoming inaccessible to memory. The only conductor able to carry traumatic memories with him is the body. Moreover, besides the fact that the trauma remains unknown, unrecorded and not transformed into a psychic event, it is not accepted by the child as truth, and is replaced by the reality presented by the parents. This is because the child prefers to renounce the truth, in order not to endanger the relationship with the parent. The price to pay is the sacrifice of oneself, the fragmentation and the loss of one's subjectivity. "Much of the unconscious emotional and mental life is mutilated, petrified, frozen and rendered dead, or at least dissociated and fragmented, with an evident global immersing of one's being in the world and becoming actors of one's existence. "The result of this process is therefore a lack of identity and existence, no past and no future. The subject forcibly lives and acts in a present which, however, is a meaningless present".

According to Ferenczi (1931), only the encounter with another person, in particular with the therapist, can allow a recognition of the "catastrophe" and its continuous repetition that occurs at the body and relational level and that also occurs in the interaction between patient and therapist. The therapist must be able to share, respecting the patient's need for reality, allowing the transition from something that did not take place to the birth of a new place, but this time with alternative and different emotional tools compared to the past experience. "Trauma does not merely pertain to what has taken place, but to what has not taken place because, in his view, there has been a lack of that place of encounter between the minds that is essential for a healthy psychic development. According to Ferenczi (1931), therefore, the therapist's objective is to provide the patient with an adequate environment that he has not been able to experience in the past, and to put an end to the repetition of that catastrophe that paradoxically is familiar, but does not feel like its own, to make it metabolized and finally swayable.

Psychic trauma and attachment theory: developments and new perspectives

The attachment theory of J. Bowlby and his collaborators represents an interesting meeting point of different orientations such as psychoanalysis, cognitive psychology, ethology, cybernetics, neurophysiology, the systemic approach that gave rise to a solid theory, interesting also with regard to psychic trauma.

Bowlby, moved by his desire to express his disagreement with classical psychoanalysis, and referring to the discoveries in ethology, in particular Lorenz's studies on imprinting and Harlow's studies on macaque rhesus, came to formulate a completely revolutionary theory, placing the concept of "attachment" at the center and arguing that the primary motivation in the development of the child was the "motivation of attachment".

The attachment system is a motivational system that involves the search for proximity to a figure identified as capable of providing protection and proximity.

When protection or safety is lacking, the child expresses his or her discomfort through protest. The caregivers have the task of providing a "safe base", that is to say, a place where they can return after the normal distances to explore the world, where they can be reassured, comforted and nourished. Bowlby writes, "I use the term attachment to indicate a behavioral pattern that is based on eliciting, or seeking, care from someone who feels less able to face the world than someone else to whom it addresses its demands.

Thanks to the studies of Mary Ainsworth and her collaborators on the Strange Situation, it was possible to demonstrate that, during the first year of life, children develop a specific model of attachment to caregivers, and it was possible to identify the different patterns of attachment. Attachment patterns can be considered adaptive/defensive strategies adopted by the child in relation to the emotional availability shown by the attachment figures towards the child during the first year of life. The Strange Situation is a standard procedure, consisting of eight phases, in which the behavior of the child in the face of stressful conditions is observed. In particular, the exploration behavior of the child and its reactions in the presence or absence of the attachment figure, including moments of reunification, are observed.

In summary, four attachment styles have been identified:

* "safe' or 'type B', characterized by a responsive and sensitive mother and a child capable of exploring the surrounding environment, protesting in a way that is The Committee believes that the separation from the mother is adequate and that it is easily consolable by seeking contact during reunification;

* "insecure-evident" or "type A", characterized by a mother who is insensitive to requests for help and comfort, and by a child who does not share the game with his parent, does not show discomfort in the face of separation with the latter and does not seek reunification, refusing even markedly physical contact;

* "insecure-ambivalent" or "type C", characterized by an unpredictable and non-responsive mother and by unconscious children at the time of separation, unable to explore the environment and ambivalent at the time of reunification;

* "disorganized" of "type D", introduced later by Main and Solomon, characterized by a mother who arouses terror and by children who show inconsistent and paradoxical behavior towards the parent (for example, by searching for and rejecting him at the same time).

Attachment styles in the early years of life have some interesting features:

* stability in the course of development, for which they have a predictive value, but not a causative one, as they can change thanks to subsequent interpersonal experiences;

* are unique and specific to each relationship the child is engaged in,

* are translated into cognitive structures first implicit and then declaratory called "Internal Operating Models" (MOI), and include mental representations of the Self, the figure of attachment and the emotional state associated with the relationship.

MOIs are the most interesting aspect of attachment theory. They imply that "the implicit memory of the child, from the first days of life, progressively synthesizes the interactive sequences in which the attachment figure responds to his attachment emotions, organizing them into generalized representations of the interactions".

Through the Strange Situation it is possible to observe the behavior of the child. To investigate, instead, adult attachment, the Adult Attachment Interview (AAI) is used, a standardized interview that explores autobiographical memories in past attachment relationships and allows to identify the "mental states related to attachment" (Farina, Liotti, 2011b). Four "mental states" of attachment were identified, corresponding to the attachment patterns identified with the Strange Situation:

* secure autonomous: coherent and objective narrations of one's own experiences of attachment, with an enhancement and understanding of all related emotions;

* distancing: inconsistent narratives of attachment experiences, with an idealization of attachment figures, not supported, but by specific episodes;

* worried: incoherent, vague narratives, characterized by feelings of concern and/or anger towards the figures of attachment;

* unresolved/disorganized: unresolved narratives, characterized by memories of traumatic or grieving episodes that are not elaborated and integrated.

An important discovery in the field of research is the strong bond between caregivers with an unresolved attachment pattern and the disorganization of early attachment in their children. "When unresolved traumatic memories come to the attention of the parents, while they are busy responding to their children's care requests, the mental suffering linked to these memories activates the attachment system of the attachment figures, just as, at the same time, the care system is also active in him or her". The figure of attachment, not obtaining comfort to his sufferings, activates emotions of fear and/or anger. As a result, the care system for your children can be interrupted by sudden and unconscious manifestations of alarm or anger, which arouse in their children strong fear. In this way, the child activates the avoidance or attack/fudge defense system to protect him/her from fear. The activation of two motivational systems is

31

created, therefore, which enter into a conflict without solution. "In the interactions of disorganized attachment, the parent is simultaneously motivated by both the attachment and the care system, and the child by both the attachment and the defense systems. In reality, however, the relational distance of the child from the "unresolved" parent, caused by the defense system, activates the attachment system, so the figure of attachment, for the child, is seen both as a source and as a solution to fear. This intersubjective situation is defined as "fright without solution", or "fear without an outlet", a vicious circle without any solution of growing fear and inconsistent and paradoxical interactions of approach and avoidance. The "outlet-less fear" leads the child towards disorganization of attachment behavior and dissociative reactions. Faced with figures of attachment that arouse pain and fear and that do not offer care, protection and comfort, the relational experience is transformed into a repeated traumatic experience, even in the absence of mistreatment. "It is likely on theoretical grounds, and partly supported by empirical data, that the MOI built in the DA is multiple and not integrated, as well as emotionally charged with dramatic experience and fear without solution. In other words, the disorganized MOI is intrinsically dissociated (compartmentalized) from its representative contents: of itself (represented at the same time as needing care, receiving care, and threatened), and of the other (represented simultaneously as willing to offer care, unable to offer it, violent, frightened and powerless)".

Liotti uses a metaphor to explain this intersubjective condition, which is that of the "dramatic triangle". According to this metaphor, the child perceives, at the same time, himself and the attachment figure as: persecutor, savior and victim. The attachment figure is a persecutor because it causes fear without an outlet, the child is the victim who experiences it, but the attachment figure is also the savior who, despite unresolved traumatic memories, can be a potential source of comfort. At the same time the child perceives himself as a persecutor, as it is considered the cause of fear and pain of the adult, the figure of attachment is the victim of this danger, but the child can also be considered the savior of the adult fragile and injured.

Attachment theory allows us to focus on the fact that what can lead to PTSD is not "the traumatic experience itself, but the fact that it induces or otherwise mobilizes a representation of oneself and the FDA in the dissociated mode of the "dramatic triangle" suggests considering traumas in close relation to affective states that have not been integrated into structures of unitary and consistent meaning concerning the relationship with the FDA. These affective states, in other words, survive in somatic states or in any case in the implicit memory of the disorganized MOI, not fully integrated in the flow of the explicit semantic memory. They can remain at a latent level of mental activity until, triggered by an event that powerfully activates the attachment system, they intervene to disorganize the integrative functions of consciousness, memory and identity".

To understand how the affective states of disorganized MOI remain at a latent level, it is important to understand what happens in the subsequent development of disorganized attachment. The starting point from which to start is "motivational systems". These systems can be seen as "modules specialized in functions essential for survival and social life, each of which is functionally independent of the other: in Fodor's (1983) terminology, the modules are encapsulated. Each module of this type, once activated, organizes the mental functions and the conduct, in the direction of the goal of the corresponding motivational system, until this goal is reached or abandoned. Motivational systems are not only instincts, innate tendencies, but they are influenced by learning. They are organized in a hierarchical way, and each level reflects the way in which they have appeared according to evolution. The lower level is the most archaic, already typical of the reptilians, the intermediate level is present in the mammals and regulates the interactions between the members of a species, whilst the upper level, specific for the man, concerns the most recent and most evolved motivational systems, such as the construction of meanings, the intersubjectivity, the personal synthesis.

Hierarchical architecture of the motivational system
First Level (Reptilian Brain):

- Physiological regulation (nutrition, thermoregulation, sleep-wake cycles)

- Defense (aggression, immobilization and escape in dangerous situations)

- Exploration

- Territoriality

- Sexuality (without couple formation)

Second Level (Antique Brain-Mammal, Limbic):

- Attachment (search for care and protective proximity)

- Care (care offer)

- Couple Sexuality

- Competition

- Joint cooperation

- Social game

- Group affiliation

Level 3 (Neocortex):

- Inter-subjectivity

- Construction of structures of meaning

In particular, children who, during their second year of life, were "disorganized" in the Strange Situation, in their subsequent development, particularly between the third and sixth years of life, adopt an organized behavior towards the attachment figure, which is called "controlling". The control strategy can be "caring" when the child activates the caring system towards the caregiver, instead of the attachment system, thus reversing the roles of attachment, or "punitive" when the child inhibits the attachment system and activates the competitive or rank system, directing interactions not towards care and help, but aggressiveness and dominance. The inhibition of the motivational system of attachment and the activation of motivational systems of care and competitive, are defensive functions that allow the child to face the distressing and dissociated experiences of disorganized attachment. Therefore "the controlling strategies reduce the possibility that the disorganized MOI emerges to the consciousness in most of the daily situations that can awaken the attachment system [...] Intense and lasting activations of the attachment system can however overcome the holding capacity of such strategies causing their collapse and, consequently, the uncontrolled re-emergence of the disorganized mental states related to the disorganized attachment MOI".

The collapse of control strategies can explain what happens when you suffer a psychological traumatic event. The response to physical and mental pain involves the activation of the need for help, comfort and care, that is, the motivational system of attachment. The activation of the need for attachment, however, also activates the MOI that regulates it and therefore all expectations of response to care. While the safe attachment MOI is a protection factor, the unsafe and, in particular, the disorganized attachment MOI, on the other hand, represents a non-protection against traumatic events and an additional danger. The subject thus reactivates the disorganized MOI, consisting of non-integrated and contradictory representations of himself and of the attachment figure, and exposes himself to a dissociative experience. "The disorganized MOI could therefore remain at a latent state of mental activity through the construction of structures of successive meaning (called "controllers") [...] These structures can collapse in the face of events that imply a powerful activation of the attachment system, but also in the face of events that invalidate them.

This path allows us to lead the disorganization of attachment to trauma and related disorders, in particular PTSD (Liotti, 2004), because "all life events capable of invalidating the strategies that control the disorganization of attachment can lead to the resurgence of dissociative symptoms and thus appear in the clinic as traumatic events.

Post-Traumatic Stress Disorder (PTSD)

According to the research, a high percentage of the population, lives traumatic experiences and runs the risk of developing a psychopathology, a disorder or psychological and interpersonal alterations, which may involve limits for the subject. The interests of clinicians with respect to the consequences of exposure to traumatic events, have led to the emergence of the concept and diagnostic category of "Post-Traumatic Stress Disorder" (PTSD). In general, PTSD can be defined as "a normal psychophysical reaction to a stressful event of an extreme nature: a psychobiological syndrome that refers to an interrelated series of symptoms, which combine to form a prolonged reaction to the trauma that affects all dimensions of behavioral functioning and psychophysiological responses.

The first studies that focused on the effects that traumatic stress can have on people date back to the First World War and, in particular, to the attention paid to the reactions of officers and soldiers who enlisted, who were anxious, depressed, heart problems and fears. This symptomatology was called "grenade shock", and it was hypothesized that the symptoms depended on strong stimulation.

Related to the roar of explosions. Subsequently, it began to be noticed that some soldiers developed the same symptoms, but without being involved in any particular accidents or explosions. During the Second World War, mental health workers were more involved in the care of soldiers and concepts such as "post-traumatic syndrome" and "war neurosis" were developed. It was also recognized that the same symptoms no longer concerned only soldiers in war, but also civilians. It was then with the Vietnam War that we began to talk about Post-Traumatic Stress Disorder, and to identify the cause in an external event. The diagnostic category of PTSD first appeared in 1980 within the DSM-III (American Psychiatric Association).

Based on the latest diagnostic classification, the DSM-IV-TR (American Psychiatric Association, 2000), PTSD is defined as a disorder related to an external traumatic event. Trauma is defined as an experience in which the person lives directly or attends an event that may result in death or threat of death or serious injury or danger to his own or others' physical integrity (criterion A1). These conditions are not sufficient for a PTSD diagnosis. A response to the event should be observed with intense fear, impotence and horror (criterion A2). PTSD is characterized by some typical symptoms that can be organized into three categories (criteria B, C and D):

* Intrusive symptoms: feeling of reliving the traumatic event through different ways, including intrusive memories, nightmares, flashbacks, dissociative phenomena, psychological discomfort and/or physiological reactivity (one or more of these symptoms are needed);

* symptoms of avoidance and confusion: attempts to avoid thoughts, emotions, places, situations, people who can be associated and can remember the traumatic event, difficulty or inability to remember aspects of the traumatic experience, reduction of interests, alienation, decreased interest in future possibilities (three or more of these symptoms are needed);

* symptoms of emotional hyperactivation: problems with sleep, ability to concentrate, easy irritability and outbursts of anger, hypervigilance (two or more of these symptoms are needed).

In addition, the symptoms should last about one month (criterion E), whereas acute symptoms last from one to three months (criterion F).

A. The person was exposed to a traumatic event in which both of the following characteristics were present:

1) the person has lived, witnessed or been confronted with an event or events that have resulted in death or threat of death or serious injury, or a threat to his or her physical integrity or that of others;

2) the person's response included intense fear, feelings of helplessness or horror. (Note: in children this can be expressed as disorganized or agitated behavior.

B. The traumatic event is persistently relived in one or more of the following ways:

1) recurring and intrusive unpleasant memories of the event, which include images, thoughts or perceptions. (Note: in young children repetitive games can occur in which themes or aspects concerning the trauma are expressed);

2) recurring unpleasant dreams of the event. (Note: Scary dreams can occur in children without recognizable content);

3) act or feel as if the traumatic event was reoccurring (this includes feelings of reliving the experience, illusions, hallucinations, and dissociative episodes of flashbacks, including those that manifest upon awakening or in a state of intoxication). (Note: repetitive specific representations of trauma may occur in young children);

4) intense psychological discomfort at exposure to internal or external triggering factors that symbolize or resemble some aspect of the traumatic event;

5) physiological reactivity or exposure to internal or external triggers that symbolize or resemble some aspect of the traumatic event.

C. Persistent avoidance of stimuli associated with trauma and attenuation of general reactivity (not present before trauma), as indicated by three or more of the following elements:

1) efforts to avoid thoughts, feelings or conversations associated with the trauma;

2) efforts to avoid activities, places or people that evoke memories of trauma;

3) inability to remember some important aspect of the trauma;

4) a marked reduction in interest or participation in significant activities;

5) feelings of detachment or strangeness from others;

6) reduced affectivity (e.g. inability to experience feelings of love);

7) feelings of diminishing future prospects (e.g. expecting not to be able to have a career, a marriage or children, or a normal life span).

D. Persistent symptoms of increased arousal (not present before trauma), such as

indicated by at least two of the following:

1) difficulty falling asleep or keeping asleep;

2) irritability or outbursts of anger;

3) difficulty concentrating;

4) hypervigilance;

5) exaggerated alarm responses.

E. The duration of the disorder (symptoms related to criteria B, C and D) is more than one month.

F. The disorder causes clinically significant discomfort or impairment in the social, work or other important areas functioning.

Specify if:

acute: if the duration of symptoms is less than 3 months; chronic: if the duration of symptoms is 3 months or more.

Specify if:

delayed onset: if the onset of symptoms occurs at least 6 months after the stressful event.

Post-Traumatic Complex Stress Disorder (PTSDc)

The diagnostic category of the DSM-IV-TR (American Psychiatric Association, 2000) is inadequate, since it cannot explain the complexity of the trauma, in particular the cumulative trauma that occurs in distant periods (the childhood of an adult patient). Moreover, this category is not suitable to describe the mental life and reactions of children growing up in failed and traumatic environments, so it is also difficult to understand what is traumatic in childhood and what specific symptoms are put in place in childhood.

To overcome these limitations, author Judith Herman, head of the Trauma Center at Harvard Medical School in Boston, coined the notion of Post-Traumatic Complex Stress Disorder (PTSDc), to describe the reactions and disorder after suffering a "complex trauma". At the same time, studies to verify the validity of PTSD symptoms were promoted by the American Psychiatric Association, and researchers at Harvard and Columbia University in New York stated that complex trauma has a different clinical picture than PTSD related to single traumatic events.

Some authors, including Herman and van der Kolk, attempted to include PTSD in the DSM-IV, coining the notion of Extreme Stress Disorder Not Otherwise Specified. This notion was not, however, recognized as a separate diagnostic category, despite the empirical evidence, because PTSD is included among Anxiety Disorders, and therefore does not fit into this category. It would be more appropriate to include it among Dissociative Disorders, Somatization Disorders or Personality Disorders. It could also be identified as a variant of Personality Borderline Disorder. The symptoms described, however, have been placed among the "symptoms associated" with PTSD in cases of childhood trauma and interpersonal nature.

The problem, therefore, lies in the fact that it is missing or incomplete, a diagnostic framework for the age of development and adulthood with regard to traumatic development in complex terms. Thanks, however, to some psychiatrists and psychologists of the American CTSN (Child Traumatic Stress Network), it was possible to create a new clinical picture, in the wake of the PTSD, called Traumatic Developmental Disorder (DTS). The proposal is to include it in the fifth version of the DSM, trying to extend it to adults.

Traumatic Development Disorder (DTS)

- Cluster A: exposure to interpersonal violence and severe carelessness

- Cluster B: emotional and physiological dysregulation

B.1 Inability to modulate and tolerate negative emotional states.

B.2 Disorders in the regulation of basic body functions such as sleep disorders, eating disorders, hyper-reactivity to sensory stimuli.

B.3 Dissociative states, somatoform dissociations.

B.4 Marked alexithymia understood as difficulty in recognizing, describing and communicating body sensations, emotional states, desires, needs.

- Cluster C: behavioral and cognitive disorders

C.1 Inability to perceive and avoid or defend against threats or excessive alarm for threatening stimuli, both environmental and relational

C.2 Alterations in the ability to protect oneself and exposure to risky situations.

C.3 Disturbances in the behavior of people who live in foreign countries   self-confidence (chronic masturbation, motor stereotyping, self-mutilation, substance abuse).

C.4 Reactive or usual self-mutilating behavior.

C.5 Difficulties in planning, starting or completing a task, focusing on a task, organizing to get benefits.

- Cluster D: disorders in the perception of oneself and interpersonal relationships

D.1 Disturbances in attachment relationships (separation difficulties, fear of reunification.

D.2 Feelings of aversion to oneself, sense of unhelpfulness, beliefs of lack of value, inability, being wrong and defective.

D.3 Sense of distrust towards oneself and towards others with hypercritical attitudes or of rejection towards the closest people (caregivers).

D.4 Aggressive behavior (verbal and physical) also towards caregivers.

D.5 Inappropriate behavior of closeness and trust towards strangers even with inappropriate sexual behavior.

D.6 Difficulty or inability to regulate empathic contact (excessive involvement or detachment in social situations).

- Cluster E: symptoms of PTSD

- Cluster F: difficulties in the overall family, social, scholastic and behavioral functioning

With regard to PTSDc, it is possible to identify a series of symptoms, useful for studying traumatic development in complex terms. Van der Kolk's proposal includes seven symptoms (Table 1.4.):

1. Alterations in the regulation of emotions and impulses: difficulty in modulating primary emotions, with the possibility of creating a vicious circle that can lead to dissociation, impulsiveness, self-harm, alcohol and drug abuse.

2. Dissociative symptoms and difficulties of attention: problems of memory, attention, ability to mentalize, depersonalization and derealization.

3. Somatization: pseudo neurological symptoms, gastrointestinal disorders and chronic pain syndromes.

4. Alterations in the perception and representation of oneself: impotence, feelings of guilt and shame, poor sense of self-efficacy, uselessness and despair.

5. Alterations in the perception of the ill-treated figures: the subjects, faced with ill-treated figures, in order not to lose their closeness and protection with them, alter the perception of these figures by idealizing and protecting them.

6. Relational disorders: fear of intimacy, affective relationships, trust in and closeness to others, use of violence, dependence or avoidance of emotional affectivity.

7. Alteration in personal meanings: pathogenic beliefs and negative self-image.

Diagnostic criteria for PTSDc
1. Alterations in the regulation of emotions and behavior: a) alteration in the regulation of emotions; b) difficulty in modulating anger; c) self-help behavior; d) suicidal behavior or concerns; e) difficulty in modulating sexual involvement; f) excessive tendency to risk behavior (low self-protective capacity).

2. Disorders of consciousness and attention: a) amnesia; b) transient dissociative episodes; depersonalization.

3. Somatization: a) disorders of the digestive system; b) chronic pain; c) cardiopulmonary symptoms; d) conversion symptoms; symptoms of sexual dysfunction.

4. Alterations in self-perception: a) sense of helplessness and poor personal effectiveness; b) feeling of being damaged; c) excessive sense of guilt and responsibility; d) pervasive shame; e) idea of not being understood; f) minimization.

5. Alterations in the perception of maltreating figures: a) tendency to assume the perspective of the other; b) idealization of the maltreater; c) fear of damaging the maltreater.

6. Relational disorders: a) inability or difficulty in trusting others; b) tendency to be re-validated; c) tendency to victimize others.

7. Alterations in personal meanings: a) despair and a sense of unhelpfulness; negative view of oneself; c) loss of personal convictions.

Other disorders caused by traumatic experiences

Traumatic experiences can cause other disorders than PTSD, which the DSM-IV-TR (American Psychiatric Association, 2000) does not directly link with traumatic and stressful situations. Among other disorders we can find:

* sexual disorders: are common in both sexes, but do not directly affect the sexual sphere, as they can originate from other factors, such as: depression (may result in a decline in desire, little erotic imagery), anxiety (inhibition of desire, problems in achieving pleasure, difficulty in maintaining an erection in men, vaginism or dyspareunia in women), distrust (difficulty in establishing intimate ties), alexithymia, personality disorders. Furthermore, sexual abuse can lead to confusion of sexual identity, sexual promiscuity, perversions, difficulties in accepting one's own body;

* uro-gynecological disorders: they can be typical in subjects who have undergone child sexual abuse, and may concern vulvodynia, chronic pelvic pain, interstitial cystitis;

* eating disorders: mainly related to child sexual abuse, but also to inadequate care by caregivers. In particular, it is possible to find bulimia, disturbances of the body image, elimination ducts;

* somatoform disorders and medical pathologies: they are associated, in particular, with abuses and forms of maltreatment, but also with minor traumas linked to the non-responsiveness of caregivers;

* anxiety disorders: social phobia may be found (underlying psychological abuse by caregivers, physical defects, puberty changes or situations that may cause embarrassment to the subject), a generalized anxiety disorder (may be related to having suffered natural disasters or accidents);

* depression: this is a very present disorder that is strongly correlated with PTSD, especially after natural disasters;

* personality disorders: it is possible to identify a strong comorbidity between personality disorders and PTSD, this is because both the personality can influence the individual, the development and the course of PTSD, both because the personality can be influenced by PTSD;

* dissociative disorders: the dissociative phenomenon may be a symptom of several disorders, such as PTSD, acute stress disorder, panic disorder, borderline personality disorder, etc., but in dissociative disorder dissociation is the central dysfunctional element. These disorders are characterized by dissociative amnesia, sudden and unexpected escapes, dissociative identity disorder (multiple personality), depersonalization disorder (feeling of detachment from one's body and mental processes);

* vicarious traumatization: this is a secondary traumatization that can be typical, above all, of the voluntary and professional personnel who provide assistance in emergency situations and who tend to put in place a repressive style of emotions;

* substance abuse: can be a disorder related to problems in the attachment bond, having been victims of physical or sexual aggression. It can be typical even in war veterans.

CHAPTER THREE:
ANXIETY DISORDERS

Fear, anxiety, anguish, panic, terror is often considered similar emotions. In particular, they have in common the feeling of imminent danger and the somatic reaction of alarm that activates the subject and allows him to face the danger through the attack or escape.

Speaking of Anxiety Disorders, it is interesting to understand the meaning of anxiety, the way it is structured and raised, and how it differs from fear.

The first theories on anxiety can be traced back to Sigmund Freud (1925) and later authors, who considered anxiety as a multidimensional aspect and not as a unitary phenomenon. Freud had made a distinction between real anguish (an innate and involuntary response to an internal or external distress situation) and signal anguish (a learned fear response with a function of warning signal to traumatic or conflictual situations). Further studies, following Freud's, then divided the learned anxiety into three forms: panic attacks (unjustified episodes of terror, in the absence of a cause, characterized by imminent catastrophe and activation of the sympathetic nervous system), anticipatory anxiety (caused by a precise signal associated with the danger) and chronic anxiety (persistent tension not related to identifiable external threats).

Specifically, anxiety is an unjustified, excessive and unwanted fear reaction to a situation that is not normally considered dangerous. "A condition of general activation of physical and mental resources, activated in the presence of something that is not immediately identifiable. The event, which apparently may seem harmless and insignificant, unmotivated and meaningless, is perceived and evaluated by the subject as frightening and dangerous, as it prevents the achievement of relevant goals.

Fear, on the other hand, is an automatic "basic" element, a primary emotion, useful for survival, widespread both in humans and animals, which signals a possible danger and prepares us to save ourselves. It includes three elements: the subjective experience of fear, the physiological modification of the organism, the system of attack or flight to cope with the threat. Fear is triggered by concrete dangers in time and space. In fact, when faced with a real danger, the organism activates itself psychologically and physiologically to face it in the best possible way. In anxiety, on the other hand, the danger is supposed and distant, negatively evaluated and considered a threat to which to be constantly alerted. Anxiety, therefore, becomes a bioadaptive signal, because it causes in the subject a continuous brooding and a continuous concern about possible future dangers, with the consequence of a wearisome existence in the present, and an excessive expenditure of energy, because, in view of feared potential attacks, the organism is continuously activated and alerted and prepared for the behavior of attack and flight, but since all this predisposition is not followed by action, because the dangerous event will not take place, it does not have the opportunity to unload and to restore the previous balance.

From a cognitive point of view, anxiety is due to a poor sense of self-efficacy in the face of a situation interpreted as threatening and excessive vulnerability, which pushes the individual towards constant vigilance and attention to every detail. Furthermore, the subject overestimates both the possibility of the threatening event happening and its seriousness. This interpretation activates escape or avoidance in the subject but does not eliminate the idea of the environment as threatening and the inability to cope with it.

In addition, this dysfunctional anxiety, which constantly commits the subject to avoiding behavior, compromises the ability to face the tasks of daily life and affective relationships. As a result, the subject, sees his life deteriorate and often attributes responsibility for lack of ability and vulnerability to himself. This assessment may lead to secondary depression, with a further loss of quality of life and a lowering of self-esteem.

Classification of Anxiety Disorders

Anxiety Disorders of Axis I of the DSM-IV-TR (American Psychiatric Association, 2000) will be considered. These disorders have in common the mechanisms of genesis and maintenance of anxiety, that is, they are supported by metacognitive beliefs and by emotional and behavioral processes that lead to interpretations and evaluations of reality and of oneself in an erroneous and catastrophic way. These mechanisms regulate the functioning of the cognitive system and are responsible for establishing and maintaining anxiety disorder. They differ, however, for the purpose that the subject feels continuously and repeatedly threatened. So, the anxiety is always the same, what, instead, differentiates the various disorders is the purpose that the subject desires and to which he cannot give up, but that warns threatened.

The DMS-IV-TR (American Psychiatric Association, 2000) identifies the following disorders in this section:

* Panic Attack

* Agoraphobia

* Panic Disorder without Agoraphobia

* Agoraphobia without a history of Panic Disorder

* Specific Phobia

* Social Phobia

* Obsessive-Compulsive Disorder

* Post-traumatic Stress Disorder

* Acute Stress Disorder

* Generalized Anxiety Disorder

* Anxiety Disorder Due to a General Medical Condition

* Substance-induced anxiety disorder

* Anxiety disorder not otherwise specified.

Panic Attack

The subject experiences a sudden and intense terror, a feeling of impending catastrophe and loss of control. According to the DSM-IV-TR the intense fear must be accompanied by at least four somatic or cognitive symptoms on a list of thirteen (palpitations, heart palpitations or tachycardia, sweating, fine tremors or large tremors, dyspnea or suffocation sensation, asphyxiation sensation, chest pain or discomfort), nausea or abdominal disorders, feelings of skidding and instability, feelings of unreality and depersonalization, fear of losing control or going crazy, fear of dying, paresthesia's, chills or hot flashes) that suddenly arose and reached their peak within 10 minutes. There is often a need to escape from the perceived dangerous situation.

For the Panic Attack it is not possible to codify a specific diagnosis, because it presents itself in different Anxiety Disorders, and therefore it constitutes only a symptom.

The Panic Attack can be divided into:

* Unexpected Panic Attack: it is not caused by any factor, so it arises spontaneously, and is typical of Panic Disorder with or without Agoraphobia.

* Panic attack caused by the situation: it manifests itself in the presence of the situational triggering factor and is characteristic of Social Phobia and specific Phobias.

* Sensitive panic attack to the situation: it occurs after the exposure of the stimulus, but it is not necessarily associated with the triggering factor so it may also occur later. It can be frequent in Panic Disorder, but also in Social Phobia and specific Phobias.

Agoraphobia
As with the Panic Attack, Agoraphobia is also to be considered a symptom that can manifest itself in Panic Disorder with Agoraphobia and in Agoraphobia without a history of Panic Disorder.

In the case of Agoraphobia, anxiety arises in places or situations where it is difficult to get away, or where help and support is not possible in the event of panic. The consequence is that the subject avoids all those potentially dangerous situations or endures them, but with much discomfort. Typical situations of discomfort are being in the middle of the crowd, travelling by car, being in the elevator, being at home alone. In addition, the avoidance attitude, can compromise all normal and daily actions, such as going to work or carry out various domestic commissions (es. shopping).

Panic Disorder without Agoraphobia
This type of disorder is characterized by frequent and sudden Panic Attacks, insistent concern about having another possible Panic Attack, and concern about the consequences of the Panic Attacks and a change in behavior in relation to the attack. Panic attacks are not related to the effect of a substance, a general medical condition or another mental disorder. In addition, subjects experience a constant or intermittent sense of anxiety that is not related to a specific situation. They are exaggeratedly concerned about their health, interpreting minor physical symptoms in a catastrophic way, thus producing a chronic debilitating anxiety. Often the disorder can be associated with experiences of loss and separation with loved ones, such as going to live alone or divorcing.

Demoralization can be frequent in these subjects, as they live feelings of shame, dissatisfaction and difficulty in leading normal daily life. From a physiological point of view, transient tachycardia and elevation of systolic pressure may occur.

Panic attacks can be moderate in frequency, e.g. once a week or daily with periods without attacks or with infrequent attacks. The onset of the disorder generally lies between late adolescence and 35 years of age. In some cases, it may start in childhood or after the age of 45.

Agoraphobia without a history of Panic Disorder
Unlike Panic Disorder with Agoraphobia, in which Panic Attacks are complete, this type of disorder is characterized by incapacitating or embarrassing attacks, and by Agoraphobia with fear and symptoms of panic (of the 13 listed for Panic Attack).

Specific phobia
In specific Phobia there is an evident, recurrent, unreasonable and excessive fear of a distinguishable, circumscribed and specific object or situation. When faced with a phobic stimulus, the subject reacts immediately with an anxious response, which can take the form of a Panic Attack. The reactions of avoidance, fear and anxiety resulting from the exposure of the phobic stimulus, clearly interfere with the tasks of daily life, work and social life. Fear can occur in the presence of a specific object or situation and may involve fear of losing control and panic. The object of fear can be animal, environmental/natural (thunderstorms, heights, water...), blood-injections-wound, situational (public transport, tunnels, bridges, elevators, flying, driving or closed places...).

Social Phobia (Social Anxiety Disorder)
There is an evident, marked and recurrent fear of social or performance situations, and exposure to the social phobic stimulus triggers an immediate anxiety response that can take the form of a situational panic attack. Here too, as in Specific Phobia, this type of disorder interferes with social, educational and occupational functioning. These subjects, faced with social or performance situations, fear the embarrassment and judgment of others, in particular the concern to be judged anxious, weak, crazy or stupid. Often these subjects, in the presence of the feared situations, have symptoms of anxiety such as palpitations, tremors, sweating, diarrhea, redness of the face.

One can speak of "Generalized Social Phobia", when one fears not only situations involving public services, but all those situations that include social interactions; this fear may entail the risk of a deficit in social benefits.

Social Phobia is characterized by low self-esteem, feeling of inferiority, hypersensitivity to criticism and rejection and evaluation through testing. Subjects have low eye contact, cold, sweaty hands, tremors and hesitant voice. They can also present problems at school for fear of taking exams, and in work for the presence of anxiety when speaking in public or in groups.

Obsessive-Compulsive Disorder

This type of disorder is characterized by recurrent, excessive and unreasonable obsessions and compulsions. Obsessions are about ideas, thoughts, intrusive and persistent images that create discomfort and anxiety. Among the most frequent obsessions it is possible to find: the fear of being contaminated (for example, when shaking hands with someone), persistent doubts (for example, if you left the door open), intense discomfort at the disorder of objects, aggressive impulses and sexual fantasies. Usually individuals try to neutralize obsessions with other thoughts or compulsion (e.g. by repeatedly checking that they have closed the gas).

Compulsions, on the other hand, are repetitive actions and behaviors (washing hands, tidying up, controlling) or mental actions (praying, counting, mentally repeating a word), put in place to reduce anxiety or discomfort.

Obsessions and compulsions interfere with daily activities and tasks, replacing useful and satisfying behaviors.

A specification of Obsessive-Compulsive Disorder is "With Poor Insight", which occurs when the subject does not recognize and does not consider obsessions and compulsions as obsessive and unreasonable.

This disorder can be characterized by the avoidance of situations that may be associated with obsessions and compulsions, hypochondriac concerns, guilt, excessive responsibility, sleep disorders, alcohol or drug abuse.

Post-traumatic Stress Disorder

Following the exposure of a traumatic event, which may involve the person himself or another person, and which refers to an experience that can cause death or serious injury, the individual can develop typical symptoms that relate to: the continuous reliving of the traumatic event (recurring memories, unpleasant dreams), the avoidance of stimuli associated with the trauma, the increase in arousal (hypervigilance, difficulty sleeping, outbursts of anger), dissociative states and psychic paralysis.

Post-traumatic stress disorder can be: "acute" if the symptoms last for less than three months, otherwise it is "chronic". When, on the other hand, the symptoms occur after a period of at least six months, then it can be defined as "late onset".

Characteristic of these subjects is living guilt feelings for having survived. They can also present interpersonal conflicts, somatic complaints, self-harm, impulsiveness, shame, despair, social withdrawal, feeling of constant threat.

Acute Stress Disorder

Following the exposure of a traumatic event (within one month and for a minimum of two days and a maximum of four weeks), the individual develops anxiety, increased arousal (sleep problems, hypervigilance, restlessness, irritability), dissociative symptoms (numbness, depersonalization, amnesia, emotional inhibition), feelings of guilt, difficulty in finding pleasure in daily activities, problems in concentration, detachment from the body, perception of the world as unreal. Furthermore, the individual relives the traumatic event in a recurring manner and constantly tries to avoid places, people and activities that may be associated with the memory of the trauma. The risk for these subjects is to develop a "Major Depressive Disorder", as symptoms of excessive and recurrent unhappiness and despair may occur.

This disorder can compromise the performance of daily tasks and the functioning of social and working life.

Generalized Anxiety Disorder

The individual presents, for a period of at least six months, anxiety and massive concern about events or activities that may also concern daily circumstances (tasks at work, economic difficulties, apprehension for the health or misfortunes of family members) or small things (concern to delay an appointment, domestic issues). It also shows other symptoms such as: sleep disorders, muscle tone tension (including muscle pain, tremors, shocks), somatic symptoms (cold, dry mouth, sweating, nausea, diarrhea, "throat knot"), restlessness, irritability, difficulty concentrating, fatigue. The difficulty in controlling concern and apprehension can compromise relationships, work activities and daily life. These subjects may also have depressive symptoms.

Anxiety disorder due to a General Medical Condition

This disorder presents excessive anxiety, as a result of physiological effects of a general medical condition. Common symptoms may include generalized anxiety, panic attacks or obsessions or compulsions. In relation to these symptoms, the disorder consists of the following specifications: "With Generalized Anxiety", "With Panic Attacks", "With Obsessive-Compulsive Symptoms".

Substance-induced anxiety disorder

Individuals experience symptoms of anxiety, panic attacks, phobias, obsessions or compulsions as a result of the physiological effects of a substance (a drug, a medication, a toxin). Among the specifications of this disorder we have that "Generalized Anxiety", "With Panic Attacks", "With Obsessive-Compulsive Symptoms", "With Phobic Symptoms", "With Onset During Intoxication", "With Onset During Abstinence".

Anxiety Disorder Not Otherwise Specified

Includes those anxiety disorders or phobic avoidance that do not meet the criteria for any specific Anxiety Disorder, Anxiety Adaptation Disorder and Depressed Mood. This category may include mixed anxiety depressive disorder (anxiety and depression symptoms), social phobia symptoms related to a general medical condition or mental disorder, anxiety disorder of which it is not possible to specify whether it is primary, due to a general condition or induced by substances.

The generative and maintenance processes and the psychopathological beliefs of Anxiety Disorders

Processes are metacognitive beliefs that allow to regulate the functioning of the system. Often the subject is not aware of behaving according to a certain rule. Therefore, what causes the disturbance is not the concrete events, but the cognitive structures of the individual. These cognitive patterns can lead the individual towards cognitive distortions and subjective representations of reality and are responsible for the origin and maintenance of the disorders. "The main problem of anxiety disorders is therefore not the production of anxiety, but inappropriate cognitive models (schemes) related to danger, which continuously build the external and/or internal experience of the individual in terms of danger.

According to Lorenzini, Chief, Stratta (2006) we can identify the following processes involved in Anxiety Disorders:

* Purposes without constructed alternatives: our individual behaviors are guided by goals, and they are organized as a hierarchical pyramid, where at the top we can find the higher goal and towards the bottom a series of instrumental goals. The higher a goal is, the more desirable it is, and the more desirable it is, the greater the intensity of anxiety experienced. When it comes to Anxiety Disorder, the problem is the lack of alternative scenarios. This condition transforms preference into an absolute obligation, which cannot be renounced.

* Avoidance: it is a cognitive and behavioral process implemented when the subject tries to stay away from places, people or situations that can generate an anxious experience. Avoidance is an adaptive factor that allows us to avoid situations that could cause us harm, but it becomes dysfunctional when used as a privileged strategy, as in the case of Anxiety Disorder.

* Metacognitive error: it is an error of assessment that consists in interpreting an emotional activation as a warning sign. This error is the basis of Anxiety Disorder, as anxiety is not identified as a warning sign, but becomes a danger itself.

* Bias and heuristics: these are errors of judgment and in making decisions, including hyper-evaluations about the occurrence of an event, the grandeur of an event, selective abstraction, arbitrary inferences. These errors contribute to creating vicious circles that maintain the alarm status.

Psychopathological beliefs are both positive and negative personal beliefs that lead subjects towards habitual ways of seeing things. They can therefore contribute to the maintenance and aggravation of a disorder.

According to Sassaroli, Ruggiero (2006) we can identify the following psychopathological beliefs common to the various Anxiety Disorders:

* The catastrophic thought: excessive assessment of risks and dangers with negative and catastrophic forecasts.

* Intolerance of uncertainty: cognitive error that leads to interpret situations of uncertainty and ambiguity as stressful, and negative events as something to avoid. The consequence is the inability to handle unpredictable situations.

* Pathological perfectionism: every error is perceived as a failure. As a result, the subject constantly avoids making mistakes.

* Negative self-assessment: fear of not having the skills to cope materially and emotionally with dreaded situations. These metacognitive beliefs lower the level of self-efficacy and self-esteem.

* The need for control: the need to keep things and events under control, with the belief and hope of preventing the feared events from happening.

* Intolerance of emotions: inability to distinguish the emotion of fear from a real and concrete danger. As a consequence, fear is no longer an adaptive warning sign, but becomes the danger itself.

* Sense of responsibility: tendency to evaluate oneself as responsible for negative and feared events and happenings.

Anxiety Disorders in the Evolutionary Age

"Anxious syndromes represent a relevant clinical problem for their early onset, the variegated multiplicity of patterns with which they occur, and the risk of psychopathological continuity in the subsequent evolutionary phases.

The definition of clinically significant anxiety in the developmental age is a difficult task, as anxiety and fear have different characteristics, both in terms of severity and limits at the level of emotional and adaptive processes and are placed on a continuum. In fact, unlike adults, it is not easy to make an objective distinction between anxiety and fear, because in the developmental age, a child still cannot adequately distinguish between what is fantasy and what is reality, so many experiences of fear in childhood, such as night terrors, fear of the stranger, fear of darkness and night, are not related to real dangers. One way to distinguish pathological anxiety from adaptive anxiety is to assess the persistence of a normal fear by referring to the chronological age and taking into account the frequency, intensity and duration of the anxiety. The objective is therefore to assess the impact that this state of mind has on the child's habitual behavior and on emotional, cognitive and social development.

According to Lambruschi (2004), in evolutionary age, as in adulthood, we can identify three types of symptoms in relation to anxiety:

* behavioral symptoms: avoidance and escape when possible, or behavior such as sucking one's thumb, eating one's nails, crying;

* physiological symptoms: tremors, sweating, gastrointestinal problems, tachycardia, facial redness, etc.;

* Cognitive components: thoughts about the possibility of parents dying, disappearing, getting sick, getting hurt, etc.

From a cognitive-behavioral point of view, anxiety in the evolutionary age is the product of distorted and dysfunctional cognitive elaborations, including hyper generalization, catastrophic and self-evaluation. These negative thoughts lead to erroneous interpretations of reality, a perception of the outside world as dangerous, and an assessment of oneself as powerless and incapacitated people. As a result, anxious children have deficits in implementing behavioral strategies to address the dreaded dangers.

According to the cognitive-evolutionary perspective, two themes connected with the development and organization of the Self must be taken into account: the "emotional development" that is built within interpersonal processes and the "processes of regulation and control of emotional states", that is, all those elements that allow to distinguish anxiety as adaptive state and anxiety as egoistic state. In particular, the anxiety disorder, would be characterized by unpredictable care contexts and by unsafe and overprotective attachment figures, unsatisfied and frightened. This parental attitude limits in the child the exploration of the environment and the experimentation of relationships and leads to internalize the external reality as dangerous and itself as fragile. The insecurity experienced by the child causes constant monitoring of the caregiver figures and excessive alarm signals at the time of separation. Moreover, the ability to regulate one's own emotional states is compromised, since the attachment figures are incapable of tuning in, reflecting and giving meaning to the child's emotions. As a consequence, the child cannot develop and organize emotional knowledge in a harmonious way. Having a well-integrated emotional knowledge of oneself and of others allows us to recognize one's own emotional behavior and that of others, to be able to predict it and to adopt appropriate and consistent strategies. When the child is not given the opportunity to consistently construct the meanings of internal and external reality, his ability to recognize, experiment and organize the emotional aspects of fear is compromised. Consequently, when the child experiences the fear of separation, which is normally an adaptive fear, it is considered an excessive threat, as it is not recognized, thus turning into a disorganizing anxiety. Faced with this stressful situation, the child implements behaviors and strategies of control over emotional relationships. However, caregivers tend to interpret this attitude as an inadequate avoidance in the face of an external danger (e.g. school). This error pushes the child away, and the latter perceives further fears of loss that reconfirm his beliefs and increase the behavior of proximity. These wrong attributions lead to a breakdown in the emotional and cognitive tuning between mother and child.

As far as the classification of Anxiety Disorders in the evolutionary age is concerned, before the seventies, childhood anxieties and fears were considered transitional and temporary conditions. Since the DSM-III-R (American Psychiatric Association, 1987), there has been talk of Anxiety Disorders in childhood and adolescence, and three categories have been created:

* Separation Anxiety Disorder;

* Avoidance Disorder;

* Hyperanxial Disorder.

In the subsequent revision, the DSM-IV (American Psychiatric Association, 1994), on the other hand, describes a single Anxiety Disorder, the "Separation Anxiety Disorder", to simplify the classification, since many symptoms of childhood are also traceable in adults. This choice also allows to highlight the continuity of psychopathology, in the sense that adult psychopathology can be explained from the age of development. The DSM-IV-TR (American Psychiatric Association, 2000) maintains the same criteria as the previous classification.

According to ICD-10 (International Statistical Classification of Diseases, 1992), Anxiety Disorders are included in Emotional Sphere Syndromes and Disorders, and are listed as follows:

* Separation anxiety syndrome of childhood;

* Childhood phobic syndrome;

* Childhood Social Anxiety Syndrome;

* Sibling rivalry disorder;

* Syndromes or other emotional disorders;

* Generalized anxiety syndrome of childhood.

Separation anxiety syndrome of childhood

The child experiences intense and excessive anxiety when it feels detached and separated from significant figures, usually the mother. The first symptom of anxiety must occur during the first six years of life and must not be appropriate to the physiological age. They are children who avoid being left alone, for example when they have to go to bed and go to school, because they fear being killed, kidnapped or damaged. They also feel a strong fear that something catastrophic could happen to their parents that could permanently separate them from them.

During separation from parents, somatic symptoms such as headache, vomiting, stomach pain, abdominal pain and excessive suffering consisting of anxiety, crying, anger, sadness, apathy or social withdrawal may occur.

Childhood phobic syndrome

The child shows an excessive and recurrent fear of objects, animals or specific situations. This is not a normal fear that can manifest itself in the child's development because of the level of severity and because it influences and interferes with the child's normal functioning and family relationships.

Social anxiety syndrome

In this disorder, the child shows excessive shyness towards unfamiliar people or situations, thus making interpersonal relationships difficult. In the face of new people or situations the typical behavior is avoidance. With family members or friends, on the other hand, they have normal and satisfactory interpersonal relationships.

Brotherhood rivalry disorder

Faced with the birth of a younger brother, an emotional disorder may arise, which may become pathological when it proves excessive and persistent and creates difficulties in social interaction.

Generalized anxiety syndrome

It is characterized by excessive anxiety and unreasonable concern, which, however, cannot be linked to any specific element.

Somatic problems, such as various pains and illnesses, can occur. In addition, there are strong concerns about themselves and their behavior, with the demanding consequence of requiring frequent reassurances. The main concerns relate to one's performance in the future, such as a check-up at school, a medical examination, or events that have already taken place such as a sports competition, a questioning or an interpersonal interaction.

In the diagnosis, it must be ensured that there are no traumatic experiences such as sexual abuse, violence, bereavement, etc. When the anxiety manifested is associated with a trauma, it would be more useful to speak of "Acute Stress Reaction" or "Post-Traumatic Stress Disorder".

EMDR and Anxiety Disorders

Based on the assumptions of Shapiro (1999), it is possible to argue that EMDR may be applicable, in addition to PTSD, also to other Anxiety Disorders, being "conceived as a form of therapy of experiences that contribute to the development of disorders and health". In fact, at the basis of the AIP model, pathologies are related to childhood experiences, stored in memory in an associative network. Past experiences influence present ones, and negative ones can remain blocked in the person's nervous system and give rise to pathological responses. In addition, "EMDR focuses not only on the memories that are involved in the development of the disease, but also acts on present situations that stimulate emotional distress and helps to consolidate the specific skills and behaviors needed by the individual in the future. "This is because the associative network of memory is complex, and we want to achieve as many facets of the problem as possible. In fact, since the past and the present are connected on various levels of our associative network of memory, the positive effects of treatment are propagated through the system, and the person can begin to react to similar situations in a positive way.

One of the first studies to support the applicability of the EMDR procedure to other disorders, in addition to PTSD, was that of Marquis (1991). The research involved 78 subjects with various disorders, including: PTSD, anxiety disorders, relational difficulties, addictions, personality disorders. In addition to the EMDR procedure, other techniques were used, in particular relaxation methods and cognitive restructuring techniques. According to the author, the results were positive in most of the subjects, except in the states of dependence and in the diffuse themes. It was, however, a study strongly criticized from the methodological point of view.

While for PTSD the research is numerous and has allowed to identify the EMDR as the treatment of choice for this disorder, it is disappointing to discover that after just over twenty years, studies that allow to support the effectiveness of the EMDR for conditions other than PTSD are still very poor.

Furthermore, as these studies are based on incomplete protocols and limited treatment cycles, it is not possible to give a definite answer on the effectiveness of EMDR treatment for Anxiety Disorders. The studies, however, although few and with many defects, have results that give hope for this type of research.

As the future of EMDR as a therapeutic method depends largely on research, it is of the utmost importance that EMDR advocates become more aware of the need to publish their studies. In addition, researchers should increase their efforts to assess the effectiveness of EMDR by comparing it with other empirically validated interventions in terms of patient outcomes and satisfaction.

Research and discussions on the effectiveness of EMDR in Anxiety Disorders

This section is dedicated to a collection of research that has sought to investigate the effectiveness of EMDR on Anxiety Disorders. The studies presented will be subdivided for each disorder:

Phobias

According to Shapiro, phobias can be distinguished in two ways: simple phobias focused on a specific object (e.g. fear of spiders) and process phobias in which the subject has an active role and the fear includes several steps and actions. Shapiro (1995) argues that the EMDR treatment of phobias should concern: overcoming fear through training in self-control (e.g., with active imagination techniques), processing and desensitization of the first memory of fear, the worst memories and the most recent memory, and finally the development of a positive future image in which the subject proves not to be afraid. In addition, process phobias also involve a commitment on the part of the patient to deal with the event, which is a source of fear, within a defined time frame.

Already in the early years, when EMDR was discovered, we find some studies concerning the treatment of EMDR in specific phobias.

With regard to individual cases of phobia treatment, interesting is the study by Kleinknecht (1993), which reports the case of a woman of 21 with a phobia for blood and for injections. After four sessions of EMDR treatment, the woman presented improvements, and was able to receive injections, in particular underwent a flu vaccination and a blood sample. The results were maintained at a follow-up of 24 weeks. A subsequent study by Lohr, Tolin and Kleinknecht (1995) on the treatment of phobias for blood and injections, conducted in two women aged 35 and 22, respectively, also led to improvements with a decrease in anxiety values, particularly for the 22-year-old woman, while for the 35-year-old woman anxiety reappeared at a follow-up of 6 months.

Ten Broeke and de Jongh (1993) presented the case of a 63-year-old woman with a rat phobia. After only one EMDR session, the patient reported improvements, and the results were maintained at a follow-up of 6 months.

Acierno, Tremont et al. (1994) reported the case of a 42-year-old woman with a fear of darkness, death and corpses. The treatment involved six sessions with EMD, without eye movements, but the patient did not bring any major clinical improvements. The failure was attributed to the incorrect use of the method.

Young and Walter (1994), conducted a study of two women aged 35 and 39, respectively, with severe personality disorders and persistent phobias. In particular, the first with a specific phobia towards snakes, the second towards moths and the full moon. The two women were treated with 2 EMDR sessions, according to the standard Shapiro protocol. The results proved positive in both sessions and remained at a follow-up of 6 months.

Other individual cases involving the treatment of phobias through EMDR can be traced back to the study by de Jongh, ten Broeke and van der Merr (1995), who reported the case of a 30-year-old patient suffering from a fear of nausea and vomiting. After only one EMDR session, the woman reported significant improvements, with a disappearance of symptoms and the results were maintained at a follow-up of 4 months. Also interesting is Hassard's study (1995), which reports the case of a 37-year-old woman, who, after a hip surgery, suffered from the fear of having to undergo another surgery. After an EMDR session, the patient reported improvements and the disappearance of anxiety, and the results were maintained at a follow-up of 6 months.

De Jongh and ten Broeke (1996), presented the case of a 35-year-old woman, with a phobia towards dentists from the age of 8. The woman had not shown any improvement with cognitive-behavioral therapy, while 2 sessions of EMDR were enough to start again to undergo dental treatments. The results were maintained at a follow-up of 2 years.

In recent case studies we have the Schurmans case study (2007), which described the treatment of a woman who had developed a suffocation phobia following an allergic reaction due to an herbal drink. For four years, the woman had received various types of treatments, including treatment for eating disorders, a short psychodynamic therapy, a cognitive-behavioral therapy, and psychopharmacological treatments, but all with negative outcomes. The EMDR treatment, on the other hand, proved to be more effective than other treatments, even though it did not result in complete remission of the phobia. Also, de Roos and de Jongh (2008) in their study, demonstrated the effectiveness of EMDR treatment in suffocation phobia. The 4 children examined showed significant improvement after 2 EMDR sessions.

As far as research is concerned, we find interesting studies in favour of the effectiveness of EMDR in the treatment of phobias. In particular, in a study by Hekmat, Edelstein and Cook (1994), conducted on 20 students with performance anxiety, related to fear of failure in examinations, and divided into two groups, one undergoing three sessions of EMDR treatment, the other as a control group, showed positive effects of the treated group, compared to the control group, and the results remained at a follow-up of 6 months.

In a study by Bauman and Melnyk (1994), conducted on 30 students with a phobia for exams, divided into two groups, one treated with EMD and eye movements, the other with EMD and motor tasks, showed that the results of the first group were better than the second. A subsequent study by Gosselin and Mathews (1995) of 40 students with phobia for examinations, divided into two groups, one group treated with EMDR and eye movements, the other with a variant without eye movements, also showed that the results were better in the first group, but that at a follow-up of 1 month they were not maintained. According to the authors, the failure of the results is related to the fact that, while in the study of Bauman and Melnyk (1994) the treatment concerned only one memory, in this study, instead, the treatment took into account past and future images, so that a single session of EMDR could not be sufficient.

The results showed that computerized exposure is not particularly effective, EMDR, on the other hand, produces improvements, in particular it allows to modify the SOUTH and VOC scores and phobic fear, but in vivo exposure is the most effective treatment, as it allows to reduce symptoms and avoidance behavior typical of specific phobia. This study confirmed previous research, which showed that in vivo exposure is more effective than EMDR in the treatment of specific phobias.

A study by Carrigan and Levis tried to understand the efficacy of EMDR in the treatment of public speaking phobia. The study actually showed that EMDR did not reduce fear.

A study also argued that in vivo exposure was more effective than EMDR in specific phobias, but the authors pointed out that it is not always possible to apply in vivo exposure, as not all the objects and situations underlying a phobia are available. In view of these practical difficulties, EMDR appears to be more applicable.

A study by de Jongh, van den Oord and ten Broeke (2002) demonstrated the effectiveness of EMDR treatment for dental phobia. After three sessions of EMDR, three of the four patients showed a reduction in dental treatment anxiety and a significant behavioral change. The results also remained at a follow-up of 6 weeks.

De Jongh and ten Broeke, in a recent article, argued that EMDR is more effective in specific phobias that have a traumatic origin, in fact the EMDR lends itself well in selecting and reworking past memories of negative experiences related to specific objects or situations. Instead, it is less effective in phobias that do not have a traumatic basis.

In a recent study by Triscari, Faraci, D'Angelo, Urso, and Catalisano (2011), the treatment of patients with phobia of flying was presented. Subjects divided into two groups and undergoing EMDR treatment and behavioral therapy respectively, were observed in both a pre-treatment and post-treatment phase. The results showed that both treatments led to significant improvements.

In conclusion, studies on EMDR in the treatment of specific phobias are more numerous than other Anxiety Disorders, but still insufficient to demonstrate their effectiveness (de Jongh, ten Broeke, 2009). As far as individual case studies are concerned, it has been shown that EMDR can be effective, as it leads to significant improvements in current anxieties and phobias, but as some researchers claim, it is not possible to draw general conclusions from these studies, as most clinicians tend to publish more successful cases, and therefore it becomes difficult to make comparisons and reflections. In the case of research, EDMR has been shown to produce improvements in a number of specific phobias, while maintaining results at subsequent follow-ups, but is less effective than in vivo exposure in the complete remission of avoidance symptoms and behaviors, and appears to be more effective for specific phobias that have a traumatic basis.

Obsessive-compulsive disorder

Research has shown that patients with OCD respond relatively well to cognitive-behavioral therapy, whereas, in general, EMDR does not play an important role in the treatment of this disorder. However, there may be exceptions, as there is evidence to suggest that stressful events can lead to this type of disorder. It is possible, therefore, to identify a causal link between serious trauma and the onset of the OCD, therefore it may be useful to do a work of desensitization and re-elaboration of the patient's memory (De Silva, Marks, 1999).

Among the studies present we have that of Corrigan and Jennet (2004), in which is reported the case of a 29-year-old woman, affected for 10 years by obsessive-compulsive disorder. The patient had not improved either with cognitive-behavioral therapy or with drug therapy. She was given an EMDR treatment, showing satisfactory results, but nine months later she showed a relapse with a strong increase in anxiety and a partial return of compulsive thoughts and behaviors, triggered by the intake of products to facilitate weight loss.

Another study by Bvhm, Voderholzer (2010) describes how treatment for OCD through cognitive-behavioral therapy does not always correspond to the most effective method. In fact, 15-40% of patients tend not to respond to this treatment, not to be motivated by it, and to abandon it frequently. EMDR can be considered as an additional method, which can eliminate these specific problems. The three patients reported by the authors, who underwent both treatments, showed a 60% reduction in symptoms. They also experimented with EMDR as a useful and motivating method, encouraged to deal with their emotions.

EMDR is therefore a useful method in the treatment of patients with obsessive-compulsive disorder, but further randomized controlled trials are needed to confirm this conclusion.

Panic Disorder

What Shapiro says in her book "May be continually traumatized by the fear of fear" is well suited to patients suffering from Panic Disorder. EMDR is therefore a recommended technique for these types of patients.

Among the first studies that investigated the effectiveness of EMDR treatment for Panic Disorders, we have that of Goldstein and Feske (1994), who reported the case of a series of patients with panic attacks who after 5 sessions of EMDR showed a decrease in the frequency of panic attacks, fear of living a panic attack, and fear of body sensations. In another study by Feske and Goldstein (1997), the authors compared a group of patients treated with EMDR, with EMDR without eye movements, and another group on the waiting list. The results showed that patients receiving EMDR treatment, compared to those on the waiting list, had reduced symptoms related to Panic Disorder. In addition, patients who received EMDR with eye movements achieved better results than those who received EMDR without eye movements, although at a follow-up of 3 months these differences were not maintained.

A study by Muris and Merckelbach (1999) attempted to compare EMDR treatment for Panic Disorder with cognitive-behavioral therapy. After five treatment sessions, patients who had received cognitive-behavioral therapy presented better results.

In a randomized study by Goldestein et al. (2000) on Panic Disorder with Agoraphobia, three experimental groups were compared: one group that had received an EMDR treatment (n = 18), the second group on a waiting list (n = 14) and the third group in a condition of relaxation, through association and relaxation therapy (ART) (n = 13), a technique very similar to EMDR with the exception of bilateral stimulation. The ART consisted of a muscle relaxation of 30 to 45 minutes, followed by a description, with eyes closed, of the scariest scene of panic. Assessments for Panic Disorder, before treatment and after treatment, were made through questionnaires, interviews and diaries. The results showed that patients who had received EMDR had presented improvements in questionnaires, diaries and interviews, but no improvements in the frequency of panic attacks and cognitive measures. As far as the comparison with ART is concerned, the results for EMDR were unfavorable. It was argued that a longer preparation course would lead to better results (Shapiro, 1999). This thesis is supported by a study by Fernandez and Faretta (2007) which reported the case of a woman suffering from panic disorder with agoraphobia. The treatment involved a preparation phase of 6 sessions and a treatment phase of 15 EMDR sessions. The final results reported a complete remission of symptoms and a maintenance of behaviors at a follow-up of 1 year.

Generalized Anxiety Disorder
The only study that evaluated the potential effects of EMDR on patients with Generalized Anxiety Disorder was Gauvreau and Bouchard (2008). The authors submitted to 15 sessions of EMDR, four subjects with Generalized Anxiety Disorder. After treatment, the results showed that anxiety and concern had fallen significantly below the diagnostic threshold, and in two cases a complete remission of symptoms had occurred. In addition, in a follow-up of 2 months, all four patients were no longer diagnosed with Generalized Anxiety Disorder.

Acute Stress Disorder
The only research that has investigated the effectiveness of EMDR treatment for Acute Stress Disorder is that of Kutz, Resnik and Dekel (2008). The authors described an EMDR operation on 86 patients in hospital. The results showed that 50% of patients had reduced intrusive symptoms and general discomfort, 27% described partial attenuation of symptoms, and 23% reported no improvement. The results were maintained at a follow-up of 6 months.

EMDR and Panic Disorder: an example intervention protocol
The EMDR is a procedure created for the intervention of the PTSD, so its standard structure, from the application and theoretical point of view, is proper to this disease. For other diseases, the intervention protocol appears to be an adaptation of the original protocol. In fact, although EMDR was born and developed especially for PTSD, and therefore for the treatment of events related to trauma and highly stressful, it can also be applied to psychopathology that traditionally has no origin in trauma, but that can still be characterized by traumatic and stressful experiences.

He describes himself in his book "Panic Disorder. Cognitive Psychotherapy, Hypnosis and EMDR" the therapeutic strategy with EMDR that can be applied for the treatment of Panic Disorder. In particular, the first phase is that of stabilization, in which we evaluate the disorder, the history of the patient, we try to understand if the patient takes drugs, we provide information about the disorder and we create the therapeutic alliance. The second phase involves patient preparation, and, in addition to the presentation of the EMDR, training in eye movements, stop signals and the creation of the "safe place", it is useful to use self-hypnosis techniques to make the patient more stabilized and ready to face the actual EMDR treatment. In addition, self-hypnosis techniques can be used when the patient, despite medication, has anxiety and panic attacks that can compromise work with EMDR. In fact, when the patient is in such a condition, it can be difficult to work on emotions, feelings and thoughts, and to relate to your body and your physical feelings. In addition, the patient may have difficulty reaching a condition and feeling of security. In the third phase, it is useful to exercise the patient to perceive and expect improvements through live or imaginative exposure exercises. These exercises consist in making the patient see a screen on which to slide and observe anxious situations. The possibility of observing anxiety situations in a protected and relaxing context, however, allows us to observe problematic and uncomfortable elements from another perspective. In the fourth and fifth stages, work is done on the choice of targets. The target stimulus should cover hypothetical future situations that may present anxiety and fear and may cause avoidance by the patient, panic attacks in past situations, and previous life experiences that are hypothetically at the origin of the current Panic Disorder. In particular, it is advisable first to work on the life experiences that are the cause of the current disorder, then it is useful to work on the panic attacks that occurred in previous situations that still strongly affect the patient, and finally it is useful to focus the work on hypothetical future scenarios.

In some patients, memories of previous panic attacks, although not related to specific traumas, may give rise to symptoms similar to PTSD. With these patients it may be useful to treat memories as if they were traumatic experiences, and to use the standard PTSD procedure. It should be remembered, however, that after the desensitization of target memories, the spontaneous reworking adopted with PTSD, can be difficult with patients suffering from panic attacks, so it is useful to identify life events to be reworked and return several times to the original targets.

We propose, some technical measures to be applied in EMDR therapy for Panic Disorder, in particular:

* With patients suffering from Panic Disorder it is useful, as for the treatment of PTSD, to elaborate a target starting from the worst moment of it. However, the free association of the patient is not continued. Instead, it is advisable to create a filmic exposure that will be first viewed with eyes closed to detect the presence of emotions and sensations of disturbance, then bilateral stimulation will be used to deal with and eliminate the disturbing elements. It is also useful to observe the history that has been created, change it and rework it in a different way, trying to generate new skills.

* Patients with Panic Disorder may have difficulty accessing emotions and sensations. They have, in fact, little or no emotion, difficulty in encoding the body and emotional world, in identifying and naming what they experience, so it is appropriate to use different strategies than the standard protocol. One of these can be to close the patient's eyes, ask him to visualize what needs to be processed and to observe himself while the situation that you are imagining happens. Access to the safe place that allows you to have contact with your body and the inner world can be useful.

* These patients have difficulty in transforming problematic experiences and negative self-related beliefs, so the use of spontaneous processing can be counterproductive. It can be useful, instead, to work on emotions through "perceptual alterations", associating pleasant sensations with disturbing events (for example, associating a problematic memory with a song or a reassuring color for the patient), and "cognitive alterations", going to arouse positive cognitions about oneself.

* Unlike patients with PTSD, patients with Panic Disorder do not need a closure phase, as there is no danger that the patient will continue outside the therapeutic setting an involving and excessive processing.

* Problems related to Panic Disorder can be traced back to dysfunctional attachment stories, characterized by unpredictable, fragile, violent caregivers. These patients, in fact, have difficulty in describing their attachment history and may present intense anger, fear and sadness or absence of emotions, perceptions of themselves as incapable and vulnerable people. In addition, the narrative may present inconsistencies between episodic and semantic memory. Through the EDMR it is possible to go and rework the patient's attachment system, to desensitize the most significant episodes and scenes in the attachment history, and to modify the attachment history, with the introduction of new caregivers and the integration of more adaptive internal operative models. In particular, it may be useful to develop the patient's capacity for "self-help", inviting him to imagine going into his own past and assuming the role that the caregivers should have played, taking care of his own childish Self. Other attachment figures that have been significant for the development of the patient (uncles, grandparents, teachers, educators) can also be used, as well as alternative attachment figures that are significant in the patient's present, such as religious and spiritual figures. It can also be useful to make the patient imagine explaining to his attachment figure how he behaved in the past, asking for alternative and more appropriate behavior in the present.

CHAPTER FOUR:
PSTD - POST-TRAUMATIC DISORDER

POST-TRAUMATIC STRESS DISORDER:

In the DSM 5 post-traumatic stress disorder (PTSD) we find it classified as disorders related to stressful traumatic events, i.e. those disorders in which exposure to a traumatic or stressful wind is listed as a diagnostic criterion.

They are also part of these disorders:

- reactive attachment disorder

- uninhibited social commitment disorder

- acute stress disorder

- adaptation problems.

The collocation of this chapter on Disorders related to stressful traumatic events reflects the close relationship between these diagnoses and the disorders covered in the adjacent chapters on anxiety disorders, obsessive-compulsive disorder and related disorders and dissociative disorders.

The psychological suffering that follows exposure to a traumatic or stressful event is very variable. In fact, it has been found that many subjects who have been victims of traumatic or stressful events manifest a phenotype in which, rather than finding symptoms based on anxiety and fear, the most obvious clinical features are neutral and dysphoric symptoms, externalized symptoms of anger and aggression, or dissociative symptoms (American Psychiatric Association, 2014).

The TSPD is associated with high levels of social, occupational and physical disability, as well as considerable economic costs and high levels of use of medical services. Impairment of the functioning is observed within the social, interpersonal, evolutionary, scholastic, occupational and physical health fields.

Some traumatic events also have a strong suicidal potential in the people affected (American Psychiatric Association, 2014).

A definition

Post-traumatic stress disorder can occur as a result of natural disasters (such as hurricanes, earthquakes, floods), but it can also be due to acts committed by man such as violence, war, terrorist attacks, forming a trauma, or an overwhelming emotional experience in which there is the possibility of death or serious injury both to themselves and to loved ones.

Scholars have highlighted the distinction between two different types of trauma on this subject: trauma with a capital "T" and trauma with a lowercase "t".

The first refer to natural disasters (earthquakes, floods), accidents, sexual abuse; traumas with the t minuscule instead are those traumas that occur both in childhood and as adults and leave a deep mark, more difficult to abandon and that brings with it the long-term consequences. For example, being humiliated in front of other people, suddenly truncating a relationship, suffering a bereavement, receiving a medical diagnosis of pathology, indicate traumas that often the subject thinks he has overcome but, in reality, can resurface after years still vivid and with their emotional load and painful.

Associated features to support diagnosis

It is possible that there may be a regression in development, such as the loss of language in young children. There may be auditory pseudo hallucinations (hearing one's thoughts speak with one or more different voices). Following prolonged, repeated and severe traumatic events, the individual may experience further complications in regulating emotions or maintaining stability in interpersonal relationships, or dissociative symptoms. If the traumatic event leads to violent death, problematic grief symptoms may occur (American Psychiatric Association, 2014).

Prevalence

A study using the DSM-IV criteria found that the life risk projection for the TSPD at age 75 in the United States was 8.7%. The current prevalence among adults in the United States is about 3.5%. In Europe and in most Asian, African and Latin American countries, lower estimates of 0.5-1.0% were found.

It emerges, therefore, that the same level of exposure to a traumatic event may produce a different probability of contracting a TSPD depending on the cultural components.

TDD rates are higher among veterans and other individuals whose profession increases the risk of exposure to traumatic events.

The prevalence of this disorder may also vary during development; children and adolescents have generally shown a lower prevalence following exposure to severe traumatic events; the elderly has also shown themselves to be less vulnerable to this type of disorder (American Psychiatric Association, 2014).

Development and progress

Post-traumatic stress disorder can occur at any age, from the first year of life. Usually the symptoms emerge in the first 3 months after the trauma, although it may take months or even years before the criteria for a diagnosis are met.

The duration of symptoms can range from a complete recovery within 3 months to the persistence of symptoms, in the most serious cases, up to 12 months and sometimes for more than 50 years. This temporal aspect is often linked to factors that provoke the traumatic memory of the event, stressful factors of daily life or traumatic events experienced recently.

Reliving the traumatic event can vary through development. Children may complain about nightmares despite the fact that there are no specific contents related to a traumatic event. Often the traumatic events experienced by children under the age of 6 are revealed in the game. They may not exhibit fear reactions in reliving or exposing to the traumatic event. Children's reaction to these events can be one of avoiding or worrying about memories, causing serious changes in mood.

Subjects who continue to experience TDD in later adulthood may experience fewer symptoms of hypervigilance, avoidance, negative thoughts and moods than young adults with the same condition.

In the elderly, the disorder is associated with negative health perceptions, suicidal ideas and the use of primary care (American Psychiatric Association, 2014).

Predisposing factors

Obviously at this point it is necessary to consider the fact that not all people react in the same way to the difficulties that arise and only some subjects can have reactions that are on the pathological continuum compared to the normal one.

There are several factors that can predispose a person more to manifest a post-traumatic stress disorder such as the extent and intensity of exposure to danger, pre-existing emotional problems, a history of previous trauma, guilt for surviving trauma and/or lack of social support.

Other predisposing factors are a personal or family history of depression and anxiety, neurosis, early separations. It is more common in women and in separated or widowed persons.

The diagnosis of TSPD involves the presence of symptoms afferent to three clusters: the tendency to relive the event, avoidance and increase of arousal.

The three requirements for trauma are: acute, unpredictable and threatening (Colombo & Mantua, 2001). Unpredictability because a trauma comes suddenly, without warning, and therefore does not allow you to prepare for the event and adapt to changes. It brings about a sudden situational change.

It's threatening and severe, not allowing escape routes.

Generally, it has a very high intensity, and this is particularly evident in the consequences it leaves to its passage.

Risk factors are generally divided into peritraumatic, peritraumatic and post-traumatic factors.

Pre-Traumatic Factors

* Temperamental factors: they include emotional problems of childhood before the age of 6 and previous mental disorders.

* Environmental factors: including low socio-economic status; low level of education; exposure to previous trauma; adversity in childhood; cultural characteristics; lower intelligence; minority racial/ethnic status; and a history of psychiatric disorders in the family. The presence of social support before exposure to the event proved to be protective.

* Genetic and physiological factors: they include the female gender and a young age at the time of exposure to trauma. Some genotypes may be protective or increase the risk of TDS after exposure to traumatic events.

Peritraumatic factors

* Environmental factors: include the severity of the trauma, perceived threat to life, personal injury, interpersonal violence and, for military personnel, being executor or witness of atrocities. The dissociation that occurs during the trauma and persists afterwards can be a risk factor.

Post-Traumatic Factors

* Temperamental factors: include negative evaluations, inappropriate coping strategies and the development of acute stress disorder.

* Environmental factors: These include subsequent exposure to repeated factors that cause traumatic memories, subsequent adverse life events, and financial or other losses related to the trauma (American Psychiatric Association, 2014).

Diagnostic aspects related to the culture of belonging

The possibility of onset of post-traumatic stress disorder varies in cultural groups in relation to the type of traumatic exposure, the impact on the severity of the disorder of the meaning attributed to the traumatic event and also to other cultural factors.

In particular, the symptoms of avoidance and numbness, unpleasant dreams and somatic symptoms may vary from one culture to another.

The cultural syndromes and idioms of suffering influence the expression of the TDPS and the series of comorbid disorders in different cultures, providing behavioral and cognitive patterns that link traumatic exposure with specific symptoms (American Psychiatric Association, 2014).

Gender-related diagnostic aspects

Post-traumatic stress disorder has been found to be greater, and to last longer in women than in men over a lifetime.

This gender distinction seems to be linked to the prevailing probability of exposure to traumatic events, such as rape and other forms of interpersonal violence (American Psychiatric Association, 2014).

Comorbidity

Individuals with TDS have an 80% greater chance of presenting symptoms that meet the criteria for at least one mental disorder than individuals without TDS.

Comorbidities with substance use disorder and conduct disorder are more common among males than among females. Children may experience post-traumatic stress disorder in combination with oppositional provoking disorder and separation anxiety disorder.

There is also considerable comorbidity between TDPS and major neuro-cognitive disorder and some overlapping symptoms between these disorders (American Psychiatric Association, 2014).

History of the disorder

The post-traumatic stress disorder was included in the diagnostic manual (DSM-III) only in 1980 by the American Psychiatric Association (APA), this seems to have been influenced by the effects of the Vietnam War with the social objective of compensating the American soldiers returning from this war and with the scientific objective of giving nosography autonomy to this disorder.

But not only war traumas could be counted among the causes of the onset of the TDPS, were also added earthquakes, floods, airplane accidents, terrorist attacks.

As time went by, scholars broadened their field of study, considering the TDPS also in relation to events of more moderate magnitude. The novelty brought by scholars to the concept of TDPS is to consider it as a psychic disease that occurs in healthy individuals following a traumatic event or indicates the possibility of manifesting itself in individuals without any predisposition.

The events triggering this deficit may be of greater or lesser magnitude. Intensity is therefore a determining factor.

A bereavement can be considered a minor event, because although it leads to a situation of considerable stress due to the loss of a loved one, it can be overcome with the passage of time and does not imply other types of stress; in the case of events of greater magnitude such as an earthquake, however, subjects are subjected to more stressors such as the fear that a similar catastrophic event may reoccur, the fear of losing their material assets and the concern for the life of a loved one.

This interpretation of the TDPS is based on the occurrence and frequency of presentation of events, however, some authors suggest that the determining factor in the manifestation of the TDPS is due to the distinction between extraordinary events and ordinary events in human life. In this perspective, the authors also suggest that there should be predisposing factors for the manifestation of the disorder in question.

Finally, psychoanalysts reject both the quantitative and qualitative characteristics of the stressful agent, focusing rather on the perception that the subject has in relation to his experience, his interpersonal relationships, his development. In this way, those episodes of daily life that, although they may seem less traumatic than a flood or an earthquake, present their pathological component in being relived and reactivated through flashbacks, triggering in the individual a sense of vulnerability, guilt, loss, shame, return to prominence.

Diagnostic criteria in post-traumatic stress disorder

A. Exposure to actual death or threat of death, serious injury, or sexual assault in one (or more) of the following ways:

1. Gain direct experience of the traumatic event(s).

2. Attending directly a traumatic event(s) that occurred to others.

3. To learn about a traumatic event(s) that has occurred to a family member or close friend. In the event of the actual death or threatened death of a family member or friend, the wind(s) must have been violent or accidental.

4. Experience repeated or extreme exposure to raw details of the traumatic event(s) (e.g., first responders collecting human remains; police officers repeatedly exposed to details of child abuse).

Note: Criterion A4 does not apply to exposure through electronic media, television, film, or images, unless the exposure is related to the work done.

B. Presence of one (or more) of the following intrusive symptoms associated with the traumatic event(s), beginning after the traumatic event(s):

1. Recurring, involuntary and intrusive unpleasant memories of the traumatic event(s).

Note: Children over the age of 6 may experience a repetitive game in which themes or aspects regarding the traumatic event(s) are expressed.

2. Recurring unpleasant dreams in which the content and/or emotions of the dream are linked to the traumatic event(s).

Note: In children, there may be scary dreams without recognizable content.

3. Dissociative reactions (e.g., flashbacks) in which the subject feels or acts as if the traumatic event(s) were reoccurring. (Such reactions can occur along a continuum, where the extreme expression is the complete loss of awareness of the surrounding environment.)

Note: In children, specific re-actualization of trauma may occur in play.

4. Understanding or prolonged psychological suffering at exposure to internal or external triggering factors that symbolize or resemble some aspect of the traumatic event(s).

5. Marked physiological reactions to internal or external triggers that symbolize or resemble some aspect of the traumatic event(s).

C. Persistent avoidance of stimuli associated with the traumatic event(s), initiated after the traumatic event(s), as evidenced by one or both of the following criteria:

1. Avoidance or attempts to avoid unpleasant memories, thoughts or feelings related to or closely associated with the traumatic event(s).

2. Avoidance or attempts to avoid external factors (people, places, conversations, activities, objects, situations) that give rise to unpleasant memories, thoughts or feelings related to or closely associated with the traumatic event(s).

D. Negative changes in thoughts and emotions associated with the traumatic event(s), initiated or worsened after the traumatic event(s), as evidenced by two (or more) of the following criteria:

1. Inability to remember some important aspects of the traumatic event(s) (typically due to dissociative amnesia and not to other factors such as head injury, alcohol, or drugs).

2. Persistent and exaggerated negative beliefs or expectations about oneself, others, or the world (e.g., "I am bad", "no one can be trusted", "the world is absolutely dangerous", "my entire nervous system is permanently ruined").

3. Persistent, distorted thoughts about the cause or consequences of the traumatic event(s) that lead the individual to blame himself or others.

4. Persistent negative emotional state (e.g., fear, horror, anger, guilt or shame).

5. Significant reduction in interest or participation in significant activities.

6. Feelings of detachment or strangeness towards others.

7. Persistent inability to experience positive emotions (e.g., inability to experience happiness, satisfaction or feelings of love).

E. Marked changes in arousal and reactivity associated with the traumatic event(s), initiated or worsened after the traumatic event(s), as evidenced by two (or more) of the following criteria:

1. Irritable behavior and explosions of anger (with little or no provocation) typically expressed in the form of verbal or physical aggression against persons or objects.

2. Reckless or self-destructive behavior.

3. Hypervigilance.

4. Exaggerate alarm responses.

5. Problems with concentration.

6. Difficulties related to sleep (e.g. difficulty falling asleep or falling asleep, or unrestful sleep).

F. The duration of the alterations (Criteria B, C, EEE) is more than 1 month.

G. The alteration is likely to be clinically significant or to be compromised of functioning in social, work or other important areas.

H. The alteration is not attributable to the physiological effects of a substance (e.g. drugs, alcohol) or to another medical condition.

Specify which one:

With dissociative symptoms: The individual's symptoms meet the criteria for a post-traumatic stress disorder and, in addition, in response to the stress event, the individual experiences persistent or recurrent symptoms of either of the following two criteria:

1. Depersonalization: Persistent or recurrent experiences of feeling detached from and as if one were an external observer of one's own mental processes or body (e.g., feeling of being in a dream; feeling of unreality of oneself or one's own body or of the slow passage of time).

2. Derealization: Persistent or recurrent experiences of unreality of the surrounding environment (for example, the world around the individual is experienced by him as unreal, dreamlike, distant or distorted).

Note: To use this subtype, dissociative symptoms must not be attributable to the physiological effects of a substance (e.g., blackout, behavior during alcohol poisoning) or to another medical condition (e.g., complex partial seizures).

Specify if:

With delayed expression: If diagnostic criteria are not fully met within 6 months of the event (although the onset and expression of some symptoms may be immediate).

Post-traumatic stress disorder in children under 6 years of age

A. In children under 6 years of age, exposure to real or threatened death, serious injury, or sexual assault in one (or more) of the following ways:

1. Gain direct experience of the traumatic event(s).

2. Attend directly a traumatic event(s) that has occurred to others, in particular to primary caregivers.

Note: Witnessing does not include events that are witnessed through electronic media, television, movies, or images.

3. To become aware of a traumatic event(s) that has occurred to a family member or caregiver.

B. Presence of one (or more) of the following intrusive symptoms associated with the traumatic event(s), beginning after the traumatic event(s):

1. Recurring, involuntary and intrusive unpleasant memories of the traumatic event(s).

Note: Spontaneous and intrusive memories do not necessarily appear as unpleasant and can be expressed as a refreshing game.

2. Recurring unpleasant dreams in which the content and/or emotions of the dream are linked to the traumatic event(s).

Note: It may be possible to ascertain that the terrorizing content is related to the traumatic event.

3. Dissociative reactions (e.g., flashbacks) in which the child feels or acts as if the traumatic event(s) was/are reoccurring. Such reactions can occur along a continuum, where the extreme expression is the complete loss of awareness of the surrounding environment. The specific ritualization of the trauma can occur in the game.

4. Intense or prolonged psychological suffering at exposure to internal or external triggers that symbolize or resemble some aspect of the traumatic event(s).

5. Marked physiological reactions in response to factors reminiscent of the traumatic event(s).

C. One (or more) of the following symptoms, which represent persistent avoidance of stimuli associated with the traumatic event(s) or negative changes in thoughts and emotions associated with the traumatic event(s), must be present, initiated or worsened after the traumatic event(s).

Persistent avoidance of stimuli

1. Avoidance or attempted avoidance of activities, places or physical factors that evoke memories of the traumatic event(s).

2. Avoidance or attempted avoidance of people, conversations or interpersonal situations that evoke memories of the traumatic event(s).

Negative cognitive changes

3. Substantial increase in the frequency of negative emotional states (e.g., fear, guilt, sadness, shame, confusion).

4. Marked decrease in interest or participation in significant activities, including limitation of the game.

5. Socially withdrawn behavior.

6. Persistent reduction in the expression of positive emotions.

D. Alteration of arousal and reactivity associated with the traumatic event(s), initiated or worsened after the traumatic event(s), as evidenced by two (or more) of the following criteria:

1. Irritable behavior and explosions of anger (with little or no provocation) typically expressed in the form of verbal or physical aggression against persons or objects (including extreme access to anger).

2. Hypervigilance.

3. Exaggerated alarm response.

4. Problems with concentration.

5. Difficulties related to sleep (e.g. difficulty falling asleep or falling asleep, or unrestful sleep).

E. The duration of the alterations is more than 1 month.

F. The alteration causes clinically significant discomfort or impairment in the relationship with parents, siblings, peers or other caregivers, or in school behavior.

G. The alteration is not attributable to the physiological effects of a substance (e.g. drugs, alcohol) or to another medical condition.

Specify which one:

With dissociative symptoms: The individual's symptoms meet the criteria for a post-traumatic disorder and the individual experiences persistent or recurrent symptoms of either of the following two criteria:

1. Depersonalization: Persistent or recurring experiences of feeling detached from, and as if one were an external observer of, one's own mental processes or body (e.g., sensation of being in a dream; feeling of unreality of oneself or one's body or of the slow passing of time).

2. Derealization: Persistent or recurrent experiences of unreality of the surrounding environment (for example, the world around the individual is experienced by him as unreal, dreamlike, distant or distorted).

Note: To use this subtype, dissociative symptoms should not be attributable to the physiological effects of a substance (e.g., blackout) or another medical condition (e.g., complex partial seizures).

Specify if:

With delayed expression: If the diagnostic criteria are not fully met within 6 months of the event (although the onset and expression of some symptoms may be immediate) (American Psychiatric Association, 2014).

CHAPTER FIVE:
EMDR AND DRUG ADDICTION

In 1957, the World Health Organization (WHO) gave a precise definition of drug addiction: "Drug addiction is a state of periodic or chronic intoxication caused by repeated use of a drug, whether natural or synthetic".

According to DSM-IV-TR substance dependence is "a pathological mode of use of the substance that leads to clinically significant impairment or discomfort, as manifested by three (or more) of the following conditions, which occur at any time during the same 12-month period:

1. tolerance, as defined by each of the following criteria:

- The need for significantly higher doses of the substance to achieve the desired intoxication or effect

- A significantly reduced effect with the continued use of the same amount of the substance

2. abstinence, as manifested by each of the following criteria:

- The characteristic withdrawal syndrome for the substance (refer to Criteria A and B of   the six criteria for withdrawal from specific substances)

- The same substance (or   a   closely   related one) is   taken   to   attenuate   or avoid withdrawal symptoms

3. The substance is often taken in larger quantities or for longer periods than expected by the subject

 4. Persistent desire or unsuccessful attempts to reduce or control the use of the substance

 5. A large amount   of   time   is   spent   on   activities   necessary   to   obtain the substance (e.g., smoking "in the chain"), or to recover from its effects

 6. Interruption or reduction of important social, work or recreational   activities due to the use of the substance

7. Continued use of substances notwithstanding the awareness of having a persistent or recurrent physical or psychological problem that is likely to be caused or exacerbated by the substance (e.g. the person continues to use cocaine despite the recognition of a cocaine-induced depression, or continues to drink despite the recognition of a worsening ulcer due to alcohol intake).

According to the WHO, drug addiction must be distinguished from abuse, which is defined as "a state resulting from repeated use of a drug".

DSM-IV-TR also differentiates substance abuse from substance dependence, defining it as "a pathological modality of use of a substance, leading to clinically significant impairment or discomfort, as manifested by one (or more) of the following conditions, which recur within a 12-month period":

1. Recurrent use of the substance resulting in an inability to perform the main tasks related to the role at work, at school or at home (e.g. repeated absences or poor work performance related to the use of substances; absences, suspensions or expulsions from school related to substances; neglect in the care of children or the home).

2. Recurrent use of the substance in physically hazardous situations (e.g. driving a car or operating machinery in a state of impairment due to the use of the substance)

3. Recurring legal problems related to substances (e.g. arrests for substance related harassment)

4. Continued use of the substance despite persistent or recurrent social or interpersonal problems caused or exacerbated by the effects of the substance (e.g. conjugal discussions on the consequences of intoxication, physical confrontation).

The most common drug addictions are alcoholism, heroin addiction , cocaine addiction, addiction to amphetamines and calming agents, to which we must add, in recent years, drug addictions from benzodiazepines and antipsychotics; even more recently is the group of drug addictions, which we could call more modern, aimed at hallucinogenic drugs. The choice of the drug often depends on external conditions or even on the type of personality, and on the desired effects after taking the drug: e.g. alcohol is preferred by those who wants a more intense relationship with the surrounding world, certain hallucinogenic drugs, on the contrary, lead to a deep isolation (Spoerri, 1962). Another motivation for an individual to take the substance is the need to "escape" from the pain of a trauma suffered, without having any awareness that addiction will give rise to other indefinite traumas. Chronic drug abuse leads to an alteration of the personality, to a moral disintegration of the individual, which demonstrates social unfitness, evident in personal relationships and work commitments. All this becomes more and more marked and soon the individual will become a parasite and harmful element to society for the example it spreads and for the proselytism that often characterizes it.

The best classification of the main categories of drugs remains that of Lewin. We must also insist on the fact that the list of substances that can be used to produce and maintain drug addiction is almost unlimited and is always open. Here is the Lewin classification, (updated):

Euphoria: heroin and cocaine

- *Heroin*

Among the dependencies that are recorded in Italy is the most widespread and devastating, even in Europe and North America, in the Third World, especially in the areas of production (Southeast Asia, Middle East). This toxic substance is characterized by a relatively rapid development of physical and mental dependence, tolerance and a defined lifestyle. In Italy, consumption is mainly carried out by adolescents and young adults who start by testing the substance, driven by the insistence of friends or peers who feed curiosity and desire to "transgress". Often the process of dependence evolves from occasional, "functional" recreational use, to more frequent regular use, up to daily, multi-day and dependent use. Others use heroin in a "self-therapeutic" context, from which a multi-day compulsive use generally ends up developing, associated with a lifestyle also centered on compulsive substance research. Heroin abuse is considered as a "downer" alongside alcohol and benzodiazepines (to counter the exciting effects of psychostimulants such as cocaine and amphetamines), in a context of chaotic poly abuse.

The method of taking heroin is initially, most of the time, the early endonasal method followed by intravenous and tendomuscular intake. The subject searches for the unbridled effect, the "flash" a warm skin and visceral sensation, physical, full of intensity that is accompanied by a pleasant serenity, a dreamy indifference. Once the desired effect is achieved, it occurs as a symbiosis between substance and living body, quickly the body no longer belongs to the subject, it is defenseless under the brutal effect of the substance.   This is how a paradisiacal reality becomes infernal, it can be a cause of sudden death. Here is the "flash" as described by a patient   of Cl. Olievenstain (1970): "...I feel the orgasm in my belly like an unbearably joyful burn. The heroine has taken possession of my body, my soul, there is no longer hunger to be satisfied, nor sleep to be recovered, an intense joy and a complete satisfaction of desires has exhausted my senses. At this point happiness has taken on a new aspect...". This example demonstrates the nature of drug addiction and how it is a regression to a primitive form of pleasure, absolute as that of the infant at the moment of satiety. A pleasure that replaces and excludes all others.

Such a sensation of intense pleasure of the psychophysical type, arises quickly, lasts little and is followed by a period of peace, of nirvana, supported by the anxiolytic and analgesic effect of the substance. The psychomotor slowdown, caused by the heroine, is also reflected in the speech; the subject, if the dose is high enough, assumes characteristic postures (in jargon, "bent"). Consciousness is obscured, the word "lowered", the breath slowed down. The histamine substances released into the skin cause itching, which manifests itself in the characteristic scratches. The effect passes in a few hours, and leaves the place, in the habitual recruiters, to ever shorter periods of well-being, followed by periods in which the subject feels in increasingly imposing terms the need to take a new dose, to avoid the agony caused by withdrawal crises.

Hence the climb, the possible criminal and anti-social implications, all complications easy to imagine. Heroin, during chronic intoxication, decreases the tone of the vegetative nervous system, more than the sympathetic, thyroid and adrenaline system, and consequently causes typical organic changes, such as dry skin, slow pulse, paleness, myosis, constipation, decrease in gastric secretion and urinary, loss of appetite and consequent weight loss, reduction of libido and menstruation, hypotension; signs of injections, skin scars, outcomes of abscesses, itching, paresthesia's, tremors, on the psychic side apathy and abulia. This symptomatology dominates the picture of craving and the drug-seeking-behavior. In the usual addict's case, the conditions of nutrition and blood supply are no longer adequate, because the person does not eat enough. Because of these dysfunctions there is a profound change in the personality: the heroin addict neglects all professional and family duties and polarizes all his residual energy in obtaining drugs by whatever means. He therefore uses lies, subterfuges and thefts without any shame.

The clinical picture of opioid "overdose" (OD) is characterized by coma, respiratory depression and point myosis. This is a life-threatening event. OD tends to occur in subjects with low levels of tolerance: critical moments for the risk of OD are those when the subject starts using heroin again after periods of abstention, for example after a community placement, imprisonment, medical treatment that has not been successful. The highest risk includes moments when non-voluntary recovery treatments or social reintegration come to an end, circumstances in which it is assumed that the lack of willingness to follow the treatment exposes to the greatest risk of relapse. On the contrary, a proven prevention function at the clinical level, and also at the population level, is the treatment with methadone which effectively raises the tolerance level of the subjects, as well as suppressing, in appropriate doses, craving for heroin.

When the drug is taken away from the addicts, a phenomenological complex is determined which goes by the name of "abstinence syndrome". It is a known and characteristic phenomenon, well identified clinically in its typical form, triggered by the suspension or reduction of a heavy and prolonged habitual use (DSM-IV-TR) or by the administration of antagonists (naloxone, naltrexone). Symptoms of opioid withdrawal are dysphoric mood, nausea and vomiting, muscle pain, tearing and rhinorrhea, mydriasis, piloting, sweating, diarrhea, yawning, fever and insomnia (DSM-IV-TR).

- *Cocaine*

Cocaine is an alkaloid present in the leaves of Erythroxylon Coca, a plant that grows in South America (Peru, Colombia, Ecuador, Bolivia) and that in local tradition is chewed to take advantage of the anti-fatigue and anorectic effects. Through various chemical processes, including empirical ones, and with domestic ingredients, preparations of different purity and title are obtained, which can be consumed in different ways, from cocaine paste, to freebase cocaine, to the classic cocaine hydrochloride powder, to the smoky crystallized form known as crack. Cocaine can be taken endonasal (snorting), intravenously and inhaled (smoking). The most widespread mode of consumption in the West is the endonasal mode, but recent forms of consumption include injecting, especially in subjects already accustomed to taking drugs by this route and smoked, crack and cocaine freebase: in relation to these modes of use are reported reactions of violent and pant clastic type.

The substance taken endonasal causes specific and localized problems. Characteristic is the catarrhal inflammation of the nasal mucous membranes (chorizema), atrophic rhinitis, perforation of the sinus   . Another method of recruitment is intramuscular injection of cocaine solutions. The abuse of this drug occurs more frequently in impulsive and/or extroverted individuals who belong to certain social environments such as prostitutes, alcoholics, parasites, etc. What the subject is looking for is cocaine intoxication, which resembles alcohol. The psychological effects of acute intoxication emerge when cocaine comes into contact with the brain. Areas that are altered are related to mood, cognitive functions, instinctual functions and level of awareness.   This results in an immediate and intense euphoria, compared to a sexual orgasm, which can last a few seconds or minutes depending on the route of administration. You have dizziness, increased self-confidence, unexplained aggression and anger. This is followed by a medium-degree euphoria, mixed with anxiety that lasts 30-90 minutes, followed by a prolonged state of anxiety lasting several hours.

Thoughts flood the mind and the person becomes "chatty", with a tangential and often illogical speech. The appetite is cancelled, but a recovery in the rebound phase follows. In low doses the libido is stimulated, the sexual performance of the man is improved because the erection is prolonged, and the orgasm is more felt. At larger doses may appear ejaculation Spontaneously. The level of consciousness is high, with an accentuated state of wakefulness that can lead to insomnia. Motor activity is accelerated with restlessness. Acute physiological effects are manifestations of the discharge of the sympathetic nervous system: hypertension, sweating, hyperpyrexia, bladder and intestinal retention, muscle contractions, skin flushes. The craving of cocaine is stronger and more insistent after recent use and decreases little by little when you continue with abstinence. Environmental stimuli can lead to strong craving for drug addicts even after years of cocaine abstinence. In the most serious cases, cocaine delirium arises, with obnubilation of consciousness, mood swings from euphoria to anxiety, tactile hallucinations, colored cinematographic visual hallucinations, auditory and tactile illusions, coherent delirious ideas; this pathological state extends for about a week. Taking cocaine can cause all conceivable forms of psychiatric disorder in practice: affective disorders, schizophreniform disorders, personality disorders. In chronic intoxication tolerance and dependence are soon established and abstinence has a hypothetical and peculiar course. Tolerance is revealed by the absence of some acute effects of intoxication, which become less intense and faster as the chronic use proceeds. Pani (1996) suggests distinguishing, in the development of cocaine intoxication, the phases of euphoria, dysphoria, paranoia and psychosis. As tolerance sets in, the euphoria is reduced: cocaine addicts generally remember that the initial use of dust provided the most pleasant sensations, but that subsequently the euphoria was no longer as vigorous as it tended to be. The euphoria decreases despite the gradual increase in doses, while the employee continues to chase the primary "high", with increasing impetus to lower results. The euphoria then fades to the point that it no longer exists despite a steady consumption of the substance. Anxiety and depression, with feeling of despair, suicidal ideas are often linked to chronic cocaine intake. The abuse of cocaine over time generates manifest somatic disorders: tremors, sweating and heartburn crises, mydriasis, slimming, bulimic crises and feeling of physical and mental exhaustion. Libido is affected and sexual performance is damaged, with impotence and anorgasmia.

The lack of cocaine identifies an acute phase lasting from a few hours to a few days, called "crash", during which symptoms emerge in contrast to those specific to the state of intoxication: depression, fatigue, drowsiness, hyperphagia, and a very strong craving for cocaine. These disorders are characteristic of abstinence and physical exhaustion. The next phase (weeks to months) involves mood lability, anxiety, anhedonia, low energy, sleep disturbances, suspicion and recurrent waves of cocaine cravings that emerge naturally and in response to environmental stimuli. These symptoms gradually disappear after months or years, but the subject remains vulnerable to the risk of relapse for indefinite periods.

Phanatic

They are hallucinogenic drugs, the "poisons of illusion" (Ch. Durand). To this group belong the Indian hemp and the LSD, is to be included also the peyote, cacti plant of Mexico, whose alkaloid is the Mescaline. The use of Indian hemp is currently very widespread also because it is not very expensive. There is no doubt that cannabis sativa, whose cultivation is easy and whose active ingredient (cannabinol) varies greatly from place to place, is not a superior toxic substance like the euphories of the previous order. For this reason and because of the low cost, the number of real drug addicts remains small compared to the number of consumers. However, it represents a gateway to drug addiction that is risky for the common phenomenon of climbing. The dried and crushed natural hemp is smoked together with tobacco. Its resin circulates in bars or sticks, sometimes mixed with opium or henbane.

The group of smokers: one aspect of hallucinogens is that they are sporadically consumed alone, but usually in groups. Hemp, at a certain dose, causes slight vegetative disturbances, sensory and tactile alterations with a decrease in vigilance and intellectual sub-excitation that releases the impulses and facilitates suggestion. At this point, illusions and hallucinations are revealed in the predisposed subjects. There is currently a debate on the reality and intensity of the danger of hemp poisoning. Some people suggest that it should be allowed to be traded freely. Two pieces of information can be considered proven: the proportion of real addicts among hemp smokers is but a number of them transit from hemp to heroin. Lysergic acid diethylamide, LSD is a synthetic product recognized in 1938 on the occasion of the separation of the constituents of ergot. It is ingested and the essential effect is to produce important and temporary alterations in perception (especially in the visual field: illusions, hallucinosis, pareidolia, hallucinations, synesthesia; or experiences of " chromatic audition"), of corporeity (depersonalization, cenesthopathy, etc.) as well as dynamic transformations of mood, distractibility, tremors, cerebellar type disorders , etc.. The hallucinogenic capacity of LSD is higher than that of hemp. However, it is difficult to distinguish when illusions and hallucinations arise from drugs or when they arise from the stimulating atmosphere of the group. According to Olievenstein these manifestations are emphasized by the subject. The same author found that 12.5% of subjects expecting LSD administration claimed to be hallucinating after injections of distilled water. As with hemp, the real danger of LSD consists in the invitation to "climb" suffered by a certain number of its proselytes, who find themselves dependent on other toxic substances after wanting, at the start, only to try a "psychedelic journey".

After the psychedelic experience, extended psycho toxic reactions (so-called "bad trips"), depressive panic or anxiety states were observed, sometimes ending in suicide attempts, sanitizations of schizophrenic syndromes at a variable interval from drug use.

Inebriants

It is drugs that give abbreviations, whose prototype is alcohol. Alongside it are ether, chloroform, gasoline, nitrous oxide and other chemicals (glues). The ether is inhaled, swallowed or injected. Addiction is quick. It causes euphoric excitement, an intoxication combined with perceptual changes. Negative effects are very frequent. It is often the absence of the preferred toxic substance that leads drug addicts to the ether, much easier to obtain and at low cost.

Hypnotics

This vast group includes barbiturates, chloral, bromides and benzodiazepines. The use of these products can be surrogate in old opium men. Their therapeutic use is anteromedial, hypnotic- sedative and anxiolytic. All benzodiazepines are capable of inducing addiction, they are usually used in combination with alcohol or other drugs. The prescription should be made with the utmost care, for short periods, taking into account the personality of the patient. Benzodiazepines stimulate psychic and physical dependence: abstinence syndrome is centered on anxiety, insomnia, restlessness, irritability. Often there are comitial disorders, which result in the course of an intoxication, and can be avoided by not brutally suspending the drug. The thesis of Le Guillant (1930) is aimed at chronic barbiturism. The "useful" dose is very similar to the one that provides acute accidents, as addiction does not increase the toxic dose. The abuse of these substances leads to a marked increase in doses, directing the subject to the boundaries of coma until seizures.

Excitantia

Lewin placed coffee, camphor, kola and especially amphetamines, methamphetamines, MDMA, or ecstasy, and various similar substances, known as MDA, MDEA, etc.

Psychotronic amines (Benzedrine, orphan, pervitine, etc.) are adopted by chronic drug addicts as substitutes or associations, as well as by young people who first seek the opportunity for more extensive and genuine intellectual performance in these substances. A number of people, after having occasionally used these substances orally, in moderate doses, see a specific pleasure in them. To maintain it, they must increase the dose and thus go on to the injections and the search for the particular exaltation of the "flash" repeated several times a day. At this point begins insomnia, psychomotor agitation, anorexia, slimming, tachycardia, continuous thirst, sometimes convulsions. Intravenous doses can reach considerable grams per day. Correlations with other toxic substances are frequent and specifically with alcohol. There is an inclination to increase group consumption, such groups can often form violent communities. Long-term MDMA intake produces structural damage to the serotonergic and dopaminergic endings, which is why MDMA has been declared neurotoxic. These amphetamines can also facilitate psychiatric (mood and psychotic) problems in vulnerable individuals. In addition, there may be heart complications.

General an etiopathogenesis:

The pathogenetic interpretations of drug addiction are different: psychoanalytic, phenomenological, social.

For psychoanalysis in drug addicts there is generally a particular organization of the personality with an arrest at a pre-genital stage, characterized by passivity, need for dependence, oral and skin fixation. The most obvious trait in the addict is the indomitable impulsiveness: the dependent subject cannot resist a state of agitation that manifests itself internally and leads him to act as a child exclusively according to the principle of pleasure.

The phenomenological analysis of the concept of toxicophobia was mainly conducted by Von Gebsattel (1950): drug taking implies a change of state which includes an extraordinary destruction of the rigid boundaries of the daily ego, and this can acquire a meaning for the concrete life of a subject, depending on individual disposition. Man, in vice lives the experience of leading his freedom against himself and this feeling lived is better than the authentic pleasure, belonging to the Self. In reality, vice is to be understood as a gesture of defense, as a way of dodging an unbearable inner void, filling it with a content that produces false results a realization or fullness of self. It is a fictitious and inauthentic satisfaction, an appearance that leaves behind a residue of dissatisfaction and that pushes to the reiteration of the vicious act.

The dysfunctional social factors that, in the condition of malaise caused by the current economic crisis, lead vulnerable people to a moral disorder remain to be considered. In such a complex and dramatic historical moment lie the favorable premises for the establishment and evolution of drug addiction; some drug addiction frequently arise in particular environments, where there may be a sort of contagion, in the sense that a subject tends to conform, to imitate examples that are presented to him or to replicate experiences that have been told and extolled, particularly in an attempt to escape from a torment or anxiety within.

SUBSTANCE, PERSON AND ENVIRONMENT

As already mentioned above, Lewin (1928) listed the most common psychoactive substances, leaving ample room for methods of intake, symptoms of the effect in acute, chronic and overdose and withdrawal conditions. In 1985 Zinberg integrated three complex factors: substance, person and environment, which would condition the possible evolution from use to dependence.

Substance

In the DSM-IV-TR eleven classes of psychoactive substances are evaluated: three are the so-called "domestic drugs", caffeine, nicotine, alcohol. There are two psychostimulants, cocaine and amphetamines. Three are psychodisleptics: cannabis, hallucinogens and phencyclidine; two are sedatives: opioids and sedative-hypnotic-quieting. Finally, the "drugs of the poor", the inhalants. Each class of substances has a specific pharmacological characterization, a defined receptor profile on which to act in place of the natural ligand (typical of the action of exogenous opioids on the endorphin system). This characteristic has given psychoactive substances the suggestive definition of "false messengers". Each substance is active on different neuronal and extracerebral systems, generating numerous effects, each of which can be desired and or unpleasant and poorly tolerated, or can perform functions in the psychic economy of the subject who uses it. For each class of substances there are different products and each of these can be organized in different ways; from this may result in different routes of intake, which ensure different levels of bioavailability of the substance, speed of action and therefore intensity of effect: inhalation (smoke) and venous route (in that order) are very effective; usually are slower and less effective the endonasal and oral route. Each substance has a specific potential for abuse and dependence, which can be the basis of a greater or lesser "additive" dangerousness. The high potential for abuse of smoked nicotine in cigarettes is well known; cocaine and heroin also have a high potential for abuse. This particularity accounts for the proportional speed with which habits of consumption are established after episodic use of these substances. This characteristic has no connection with the medical and toxicological risk of the substances, so that substances with a high additive capacity have relatively little pathogenic potential, such as heroin, whose only element in this sense is the risk of respiratory depression, while all the rest of the associated pathology is linked to the route and context of intake.

Person

The biological singularities coming from the genetic structure of the person have a role in the development of drug addiction. To confirm this, genetic epidemiology studies have been carried out on genealogical trees, on heterozygous and homozygous twins, on subjects with drug addicted biological parents subsequently adopted by other families. These studies demonstrate a significant weight of the genetic factor. The inherited factors involved in the addiction would be many, they emerge in conditions of clinical-behavioral vulnerability, i.e. an inclination that evolves negatively along the e way, from use, abuse, dependence. Molecular biology studies are beginning to find genetic factors expressive of such vulnerability. This was then described by scholars belonging to different orientations, each in their own epistemological perspective, as "Weakness of the Ego"; as a tendency to search for sensation and novelty; as a propensity to replicate the effects of reward; as self-medication of stages of psychic suffering. Possible personal psychological risk factors vary according to age. At around 4-6 years of age, pathological aggression, disorder and of attention and hyperactivity, deficits in reward deferral and/or isolation- shyness may be personal psychological risk factors. Among the 7-11 years there are various disorders that can be considered risk factors, in addition to those already listed, such as: conduct disorder, challenging companions, tendency to risk, impulsiveness, lack of cooperation, maladaptive coping, anxiety. Among the 12-19 years of age there is, in addition to the aforementioned disorders, the search for novelty, depressive disorder, mood disorder and anxiety disorders. According to the DSM-IV-TR, subjects diagnosed with conduct disorder at the age of 18 years could be considered as suffering from antisocial personality disorder, and it is the latter that often plays a central role in the evolution of dependence.

Environment

Under this title are concentrated the family, the small group, the largest society, also understood as a historical environment that defines a cultural and legal framework. Studies outline the family influences on life habits, both in the sense of sobriety and abuse, and in both directions; the influences of the peer group, often demonized in the analysis and prevention initiatives is as "exorcised" because it is often considered the main cause of conditioning and relapse, but sometimes also exploited in its positive potential. The environment (neighborhood, school, etc.) is often recognized as a factor influencing behavior. One of the environmental factors is the practical availability of the substance, which is of fundamental importance in practice. It is necessary not to lose sight of the totality: the factors influence each other and interact. The analyses that exacerbate only one of the many factors are approximate: weakness of character, inadequate family, foolish environment, misery, excessive availability of money, lack of values, discomfort. In reality, such analyses cover everything and the opposite of everything. Instead, it is necessary to think, ponder and relate the different factors. The phenomenon of the use of substances is varied in quantity and quality, different factors interact in determining its development, equal importance have factors inherent to the substances, the person who uses them, the environment in which the interaction between person and substance occurs.

NEUROBIOLOGY OF SUBSTANCE USE AND THE INTIMATE NATURE OF THE DISORDER

Numerous studies since the 1980s, carried out by scholars such as Wise and Bozarth (1984), have made it possible to take decisive steps in the definition of the pathophysiology of the use of substances. The common biological effect of all psychoactive substances (with the exception of hallucinogens) consists in the release of dopamine in the cortical part ("shell") of the nucleus accumbent by meso-limbic dopaminergic neurons.

This phenomenon is the biological correlator of the sensations of pleasure deriving from the use of substances. The excess release of dopamine in the synaptic space of the nucleus accumbent is produced by mechanisms that differ from substance to substance. Clearly, each substance, which also determines the desired sensation of pleasure, through the activation of this neuronal circuit (called the "reward system"), also has other points of attachment in the CNS, and the related affects together configure the specific syndrome that distinguishes its intake. It is evident that psychoactive substances act by interacting, in the brain system of reward, with physiological substances that relate the sensations of pleasure related to vital functions: food, sex, exploration. This specifies the many behavioral interactions between substance use and such physiological and ethological functions. The powerful effects of the substitution of chemicals introduced from outside, without biological limits, at the chosen time, compared to natural substances produced in a physiological measure and as a result of natural stimuli marked over time generate neurological upheaval and behavior summarized in the term: drug addiction. The use of psychoactive substances produces a biological memory, which becomes with the evolution from use to habit, a maintenance factor of the same at the origin of the chronic and recurrent nature of the disorder.

In the case of cocaine, the main neurotransmitters involved are dopamine and the noradrenaline. Cocaine readily blocks the e re-uptake of the dopamine in the presynaptic nervous terminal. The reuptake mechanism is the main mechanism designated for the abolition of the synaptic action of dopamine, so the blocking of this mechanism has the result of extending the duration of action of dopamine and enhancing its pleasant effect. The brain areas primarily involved in dopaminergic functions that regulate emotional functions and the integration of perception, emotions and thought are the hypothalamus, the limbic system, the nuclei of the base and the reticular system. These systems have multiple relationships with the cortical and subcortical areas responsible for the coordination of cognitive functions (thought, memory, etc.) and behavior. As far as noradrenergic transmission is concerned, the effects of cocaine are similar to those of drugs on dopamine. In particular, it can be observed that in the acute phase it stimulates, while chronically depresses activity: state of hypervigilance, arterial hypertension, tachycardia, mydriasis, vasoconstriction and tremors in the acute phase; in the chronic phase, sleep disorders, energy, loss of libido, depression with possible ideas of suicide, difficulty in concentrating. In heroin dependence the most important role in the reinforcing effect involves brain structures such as the amygdala and the nucleus accumbent. The decisive neurotransmitters of the reinforcement mechanism are dopamine, opioid peptides, serotonin, GABA, glutamate, cannabinoids and norepinephrine, all of which are more or less directly involved in the action of diacetylmorphine on the central nervous system. For heroin, too, the problem of vulnerability closely affects the onset of addiction, since some individuals present at first contact with opioids with specific alterations of the dopaminergic system and the opioid system (Szeto et al. 2001; De Vries et al., 2002), such as to make them more at risk for the onset of addiction behavior. Substance dependence is considered a chronic and relapsing disease, coming from the expanded intake of psychoactive substances, characterized by a laboriously controllable impulse to repeat such intake, supported by an irresistible desire (craving), from which come behaviors aimed or not aimed at satisfying the impulse (drug-seeking behavior). The most secret nature of addiction is craving, the uncontrollable desire to take advantage of drugs, which dominates any other condition and consideration, producing substance seeking behavior. The existence of the person focuses on the need for substance, the use becomes vital, replaces other needs and upsets the pre-existing system of values. Depending on the personal and social characteristics of the subject, the value system may take on different aspects. The craving and drug-seeking condition of a cocaine-dependent, socially stable person who has the means to provide himself with the substance and to have recourse to appropriate remedies when he decides to stop is clearly different from that of a person living on the street, in precarious personal conditions (illness, pregnancy, malnutrition) or social conditions (lack of housing, income) who desperately seeks any toxic substance in order to achieve that feeling of well-being in another way impossible to achieve. The social and health consequences of substance dependence thrive as use progresses. The lifestyle "centered on the search for substance", exclusive to addiction, opens up inconsistencies in the life of the person. In the initial stages it will tend to use the substance to such an extent that the discomfort caused by these contradictions is kept under control. It may then happen that the very discomfort that comes from this contradiction, combined with the desire for and change (inner fracture, or discrepancy, Festinger, 1973), determines the processes that lead to treatment and with great difficulty to healing. In the drug- seeking-behavior, and what follows in practical terms, a halo of negative judgment proliferates around the dependent person, like a label, a mark that weighs on the subject. Moreover, the idea that this problem extends, between the two extremes of weakness of character and the unbridled search for pleasure, generates the idea that the use of substances is a moral vice, reprehensible behavior, possibly to be condemned. These positions are in stark contrast to the medical conception of the problem, which is a necessary precondition for any therapy.

THE CORPOREITY IN THE DRUG ADDICT

Husserl (1931), has given strong relevance in his studies to the role and characteristics of consciousness. According to the scholar, it is composed of a "flow of experiences" that lead to things by giving it a sense. According to the founder of phenomenology, the body has different ways of being which coexist, the Kvrper and the Leib. The Kvrper, the "body I have", represents the physical, somatic body, the body-observed in the mirror, touched, smelled or even the dead body, the body studied by anatomy, physiology and experimental sciences. On the other hand we have the Leib, not a tangible object that ends with the cutaneous barrier like the Kvrper, the Leib is the living body, "the body I am", is the body itself characterized by intentionality, transcendence, lived in its entirety not in its individual parts. Fundamental is the dimension of the other, of coexistence, the body in relation that "weaves a network of intentional threads" with other bodies. These very distinct instances designate a healthy subject when body and soul coincide with harmony; on the contrary, in psychopathology the somatic and psychic spheres take on different forms, may overlap or be divided. This is how Martinotti writes (2009), "when the separation between Kvrper and Leib reaches a clear separation, it appears as a set of assembled flesh and bones, devoid of any specific meaning, in front of which one cannot do anything but, in a terrifying atmosphere, question oneself with perplexity, looking for more or less plausible explanations".

In the drug addiction experience, the body plays a major role both on the positive side, when the ecstasy of the intake causes immense pleasure involving all the senses, and in the "negative" side, where the size of the body emerges in the tragedy of the abstinently symptomatology.

Martinotti (2009) also exposes the problematic reality of drug addicts, detecting the   phenomenological   aspect of the body   in the   addiction   to   toxic substances. The clear disjunction between the two instances, Kvrper and Leib, does not allow these subjects the mentalization, that is the mental representation of the emotional and corporeal experience of the somatic-emotional components, thus producing the search for the substance as a tool to reconstruct the original homogeneity. In drug addiction the body symptom is to be interpreted as the communication of a message that never reached the mental, which was like a short circuit in the soma, never differentiated from this as a psychic representation. The thought of the addict is hypo symbolized, characterized by a weak and immature ego. In it we see the defeat of emotional life, which is placed outside the area of the symbolic, devoid of value, without a latent content, a situation in which the psychic is subject to the body "Soma-psychotic" theory, pointing out how the failure of mental functions can affect the body in a pathogenic way. Think of the sensory and emotional data that, according to Bion (1970), weigh on the mind as "beta elements" that, if not transformed by the mental function alpha in alpha elements reclaimed, accumulate and appear disturbing for the proper psychic functioning. This could be linked to the difficulties of the addict in verbalizing emotions and in giving them meaning, emotions that can be particularly overwhelming, perhaps more intense than the healthy person. Alexithymia is, in fact, typical in drug addicts and tends to assume its own   particular   psychological   characteristics. Intoxication   tends   to   replace   emotional   experiences   with   sensory experiences, identifiable only in the two extremes of well-being and malaise, according to a binary code of reading, hyper simplistic, capable   of   deciphering   the whole   reality. The drug addict's pack becomes the only way to stage psychic disorders, from discomfort to pathology. Furthermore, in the case of toxicomania substances, action is fundamental, which is expressed mainly by means of a specific conduct, which is that of taking the substance until the desired effect is achieved and when it ceases, the toxicomania can only repeat the process.

Moving the attention to a more specific field, such as that of new substances of abuse, we see how these are often taken by the subject with the aim of increasing their physical endurance (just remember the "dance drugs"), to stimulate the somatic dimension, almost to want to free it from the control of the mental, to the dizziness and confusion that determines the complete detachment mind-body to the extreme pathological episodes of depersonalization induced by MDMA, LSD and other hallucinogens.

The experience of the high is phenomenologically referable, as the achievement of a condition of consciousness at the limit, in a chiaroscuro state totally inscribable in the indefinite dimension of consciousness. Taking the substance is the only aim and desire of the addict, it pushes the dependent subject to act, to do anything to satisfy this uncontrollable impulse. The addict is a slave to the substance, a mistress who dominates the entire existence of the subject without mercy. The unconscious desire to destroy oneself is stronger than the desire for freedom, than being the master of one's own life. Abusing of the substance, momentarily deludes, gives a feeling of freedom and peace with oneself and with the world, but the rapidity with which it disappears leaves despair and anguish. The awareness of being succubus, slaves, now far from that much desired freedom, the evidence of no longer being able to fight alone, leads these subjects to fall more into despair. It is from such despair, though aware, that the substance addict can resume his life. Traumas of all kinds can mark the life of the addict, in the next chapter will be described several clinical cases of both sexes, which to escape a past full of suffering have decided to "ask for help" to the heroine rather than any other drug. There are many researches on the subject carried out in Italy as on the other side of the world. The peculiarity will be precisely in the way in which different employees approach a specific recovery treatment, or EMDR.

CHAPTER SIX:
THE EMDR IN THE THERAPEUTIC AND REHABILITATIVE PATHWAYS OF PATIENTS WHO ARE ABUSERS OR ADDICTED TO DRUGS

Eye Movement Desensitization and Reprocessing (EMDR), as described in the first chapter, is a clinical method developed by Francine Shapiro (1987) who observed on herself that eye movement seemed to reduce the stress caused by traumatic memories. Many studies have been conducted to evaluate the effectiveness of the EMDR method, recognizing it as evidence-based for the treatment of post-traumatic stress disorder. Neuropsychological studies suggest that trauma and stress can produce important changes in the brain that predispose the subject to a high risk of drug abuse behavior. The literature shows that there can be a high comorbidity between PTSD, complex PTSD and addiction, while, in fact, the protocols in use for the treatment of drug addiction do not provide for the simultaneous treatment of post-traumatic stress disorder, traumatic   events   in   general   and   addiction. In this sense, it is assumed that EMDR can be an effective method to treat both addictive behavior and related traumas simultaneously. As with trauma, EMDR would help to reduce addiction disorders by leading the individual to progressive neurophysiological balance and trauma resolution, but it must be carefully integrated into the treatment of addiction. However, the EMDR cannot in any way be applied rigidly but must be "customized" according to the history and the personological problems underlying the dependence. The objectives of the therapy are the management of craving, the growth of self-esteem, the reduction of anxiety, anger, shame and guilt, all emotions that pervade the addict. The assumption of the substance, as   mentioned above, causes gratification and positive feelings, then   negative feelings, such as shame and guilt, creep into the minds of the subjects and this will help to reduce patients' self-esteem and self-efficacy. The drug assumes the function of emotional control and helps to make those who take it feel completely helpless. Thus, the psychoactive substance becomes a defense against, for example, not reflecting or not rethinking the traumatic event full of unsustainable consequences and negative feelings.   For this reason, it   is essential   to   act   on   the   resolution   of "frozen" traumatic memory, on   emotions   and   related   feelings, often unlikely, and, simultaneously, to   incite   the self-esteem   of   patients. The first step of the EMDR method, for the treatment of individual suffering from chemical dependence, is to arrive at an accurate diagnosis, thanks to the formulation of some hypotheses about trauma and dysfunctional patterns of conduct.   The positive therapeutic relationship, followed by a detailed collection of information on the patient's experience, will lead to a specific diagnosis, all   this   is   essential   for   the   proper   conduct   of   therapy · with   EMDR.   In dependency, a careful evaluation of traumatic   experiences and how the effects of such traumas have manifested themselves in the life of the person is necessary. Clinicians need to know, in depth, the patient's history of substance abuse, including the type of substance used, relapses, symptoms associated   with   substance use, social   withdrawal   and   periods   of abstinence.   Experts then assess the extent to which the use of the substance has affected a person's life in terms of personal or working relationships. It is also important to assess why the subject seeks treatment at that time. Potential complications related to secondary gain should also be defined. This, as stated above, is essential to deal with treatment with dependent subjects. A proper diagnosis, therefore, includes:

1. Identify the presence of dissociative disorders and symptom-based traumas.

2. Evaluate and deal directly with speeches about secondary earning.

3. Educate and prepare the patient for treatment with EMDR, assessing the patient's ability to handle a high emotional burden.

4. Evaluate the patient's ability to stop compulsive behavior and destructive because otherwise it would be difficult to bring out painful feelings related to the underlying trauma; if the patient stops using the substance the recovery will be faster.

Much research focuses on EMDR as a treatment for substance dependence, and several studies have the limit of being "individual cases" or having small samples. Most of what researchers publish about EMDR and dependence is clinical reports or clinical cases. Some scholars have indicated that EMDR is a powerful tool for the rehabilitation and social rehabilitation of drug addicted patients, when used correctly by highly trained professionals. Research can be defined as direct field experience, where the sample can vary from one to a dozen subjects within clinics or in Drug Services (SerT). It should be noted that the EMDR approach is not improvised but must be learned through special courses, which allow you not to make serious mistakes   to the detriment of people who trust the professionalism of the therapist. The analysis of the literature has revealed the use of some EMDR protocols adapted for the treatment of addictions. While the standard protocol is used to solve traumatic memories, the adapted protocols aim to treat specific aspects of various behavioral disorders, such as drug addiction. There is a specific protocol in the treatment of drug addiction with EMDR, in other words to act on the effects of trauma and on the relationship with addiction. The trauma or traumas, triggering factors, abstinence sensation (physical, discomfort) are reworked   through the desensitization of them   and, at the same time, new objectives are installed. These objectives allow the patient to function in a positive way, the relapses are not considered failures, but opportunities to understand, have information and understand what generated them. The EMDR protocol specific to drug addiction, therefore, includes:

- Motivation level of the patient: how much is motivated from 0 to 100 to -eliminate dependence

- Patient history: traumatic events from childhood to adulthood

- History of addiction: models, first time etc. It is necessary to dig to the root of the problem, what creates addiction

- Positive resources: through visualization, imagine yourself free from dependence in the future, and the advantages if you did not have dependence

- Factors triggering write in a diary the moments when it is most prone to addictive behavior, the feeling of discomfort that lead to the assumption of the substance.

The EMDR identifies one or more triggering factors that cause discomfort and acts on each of them allowing the subject to manage their lives relying on their positive resources, on their ability to resilience. Popky (2003) proposed a further alternative EMDR protocol for the treatment of addictions: The De-Tur model (Desensitization of Triggers and Urge Reprocessing). The De-Tour model is a protocol, currently very much used, which allows to process stimuli and disturbing events related to drug addiction and at the same time strengthen positive aspects of the Ego so that the subject can also be able to deal with the underlying PTSD. The method proposed by Popky starts from the installation of positive personal resources and the strengthening of these through bilateral eye stimulations (SBL) to continue the treatment through the identification of the factors that trigger the compulsion (protocol DSRC-Desensitization of Stimulus and Re-elaboration of Compulsion) and their desensitization and finally installing a "positive state " of the Ego for each triggering factor . The patient, accompanied by the therapist, tries to identify and develop resources, both internal and external, to promote change. Then the work shifts to the desensitization of those stimuli that trigger the patient's abusive behavior. Briere (1989) stated that the personality of a sexually abused child is induced to victimization and thus to adapt to dysfunctional behaviors. Examples of such dysfunctional adaptation are behavior of avoidance, negativity, repression, chronic perception of danger, hatred towards oneself. A clinician needs to know how the patient behaves in front of moments of blockage caused by painful and disturbing memories and when such behaviors become ineffective and lead the patient to feel flooded by such feelings or memories. In addition, the clinician should consider that different aspects of trauma, such as the emotional   y charged experience, may be inaccessible to patients. Braun (1988) suggested that a memory is composed of emotions, behaviors, sensations, knowledge and that one or more of these components could be dissociated and thus inaccessible to the subject. A careful evaluation of trauma considers dissociative aspects of experience. Often, patients with a long history of failed therapeutic treatments, suffer from a previous dissociative disorder. Such individuals will improve when they accept the presence of an ego alteration and agree to cooperate with their internal parts marked by trauma, and especially striving to maintain abstinence, which is fundamental to the therapeutic program. The EMDR method requires that properly trained clinicians recognize that unresolved trauma is the cause of initiation and maintenance of substance abuse or addiction. Carnes 1993 recognized precisely, thanks to his research, that unresolved traumas were frequently associated with addictive behaviors including physical dependence. He proposed 8 dimensional models integrating them into research in the area of addiction and trauma, and suggested that clinicians needed to accurately evaluate the patient's behavior with respect to:

- Trauma response

- Reiteration of trauma

- Liability

- Shame

- Pleased to meet you

- Blocking

- Separations

- Abstinence

The substance abuser is often conditioned by a lack of self-esteem, often inappropriate models contribute, negatively and dysfunctional, to the emotional development of the subject at a young age. The effects caused by trauma by dysfunctional models induce the subject to the need to treat himself and, self-care is the substance. EMDR is used to rework childhood or young age traumas, supporting the patient, giving him a functional conception of past events and current and future behavior. The effects of the treatment are very rapid, and, during an individual session, the therapist can testify that the method allows a shift of altered cognitive structures, the EMDR, therefore, accelerates the assimilation of positive beliefs, and the reworking of the trauma. The consequence is greater positive self-knowledge, new coping skills and more functional and adaptive behavior. To achieve better therapeutic effects, the patient should first be stabilized, involved in support groups, which refer to the 12 Steps, and remain sober for a sufficient period of time to avoid withdrawal and withdrawal symptoms. EMDR treatment for addiction is valid and effective when honest patient collaboration is in place. This commitment to follow the treatment starts from the awareness that the drug makes the life of the person unmanageable and complicated. Patients who are really motivated to change, to improve, can complete their recovery treatment even in rather short periods of time. Lovern (1991), indicated that often some patients, who seem to fulfill their commitment, and therefore respecting compliance, do so in reality superficially, because they continue to believe, perhaps unconsciously, that they can manage their lives even by taking drugs. These patients believe that, thanks to EMDR treatment, their lives would have been easier and more manageable, even if they had been abusing drugs. It is important to highlight the value of honesty in therapeutic collaboration, as it is not the only requirement for proper treatment in substance abuse with EMDR, but it is a prerequisite for any psychotherapy. It is important that the clinician knows, as already mentioned, the history of the patient's life. A thorough history is essential in the therapy, so you can identify any problems related to past traumatic experiences, or recent events that are emotionally unsustainable, which may suggest a likely relapse. Patients may have difficulty completing or following with participation the treatment because of:

- Fear of losing their only source of identity

- Losing the peer group

- Lose the resources of self-medication that allow him to overcome and fight against anguish

- Experience sense of security and passenger power

The clinician could identify the strategy necessary for cognitive recovery which could include alternative group support. EMDR is used to bring out the patient's emotions characterized by ambivalence or resistance. The exercise of the "Safe Place" and the development of personal resources can also be undertaken in the very early stages of the intervention program, when the patient may not yet be "stable" enough to deal with a specific work on the trauma. It is clinically useful to identify the specific event characterizing the patient's self-destructive behavior and the dysfunctions present in the body. The processing of the unresolved trauma allows access to many unconscious emotions, which allows the patient to deal with the high levels of emotional load that could, initially or permanently, be the cause of relapses or interruption of treatment.

For this reason, it is necessary to inform the patient of what EMDR is and what benefits it will bring to his or her life. This often results in a faster and more lasting recovery process in the most motivated subject. It is important to emphasize that intervention on addictions to substances with EMDR, like all psychological and non-psychological therapies, is only effective with clients who have been able to establish a relationship of trust with the therapist, a therapeutic alliance, and who have demonstrated the ability to benefit from the treatment.

Currently, few studies have been conducted on EMDR-related dependencies, especially in Italy. In fact, the e following research will be reported, still in progress, which provides for the use of EMDR as an integration to the standard protocols for the treatment of addictions in a public facility. Other international studies by Shapiro, Vogelmann-Sine & Sine (1994) will also be presented. Through their contribution, they have improved the lives of patients with past trauma and an unmanageable present. In the thesis work will be described some clinical cases, of both sexes, extracted from the research just mentioned, paying attention to how subjects react during the phases of the EMDR protocol, adapted for addiction, and how effective and valid in a very short time. The words will be full of confidence, security, and self-esteem accompanied by functional behaviors, such as abstinence from psychoactive substances, which will reveal the potential of EMDR.

INTERNATIONAL STUDIES

Francine Shapiro, Vogelmann, Sine & Sine in 1994 carried out a research centered on the demonstration that the EMDR treatment, addressed to subjects with drug addiction and with diagnosis of PTSD, is really effective and much faster than other treatments. The research includes the description of some clinical cases and from this study will be extracted the clinical case of J. (not the real name). J. like other subjects who participated in the research, was adequately prepared and informed about what EMDR consists of and how important it can be, for the proper success of therapeutic treatment, not to take substances during therapy. To ensure abstinence, patients had to perform regular urine tests. Another indispensable factor is the therapeutic alliance, the relationship of trust and collaboration between therapist and patient, it is the foundation of the treatment. The couple must work towards a single goal: to process the traumas underlying the chemical and psychological dependence in order to get rid of the drug. As already mentioned, for the scholars mentioned above, it will be necessary for the patient to participate in group therapy sessions as well.

J.'s clinical case.

In the following case, the integration of the adapted EMDR protocol into the treatment of psychoactive substance dependence in clinical practice is explained. In the case of J., EMDR is used intermittently throughout the treatment to resolve ambivalence, traumatic memories underlying current disorders, possible relapse, seizures, and still allow the patient to perform more appropriate and functional behaviors, including abstinence from drugs.

History

J. is 34 years old, was born into a family of 5 members, and he was the oldest of 3 brothers. From J.'s story it is important to underline the patient's difficulty in bringing out his emotions and his inability to insight. The patient was rigidly educated, especially from the point of view of emotional regulation. His parents prevented him from expressing his moods from childhood, especially his negative ones, because J. had to set an example for his little brothers. No one in the patient's family communicated their feelings. If J. had shown sadness or anger, his father would have got angry and physically punished him, he had to be responsible and adult because both parents were working outside. J. although he was little more than a child, he had to take on many responsibilities, acting as a "parent" for his younger siblings, when the mother and father were absent. During the psychotherapeutic session, the patient stated that although he performed correctly and responsibly what his parents were asking for, he never received any gratification, no one ever told him "good, I'm proud of you". Parents did not consider poor J.'s emotions and above all they had never seen him as a child in need of love and care, so he began to feel invisible and unimportant. For example, he said at an interview that during the afternoons of his childhood, he often sat outside in the garden, but no one noticed his absence. He lived in the constant fear of being criticized and scolded, he told in the session that he had been punished, severely in brutal ways, many times for the mistakes made by his brothers, and this generated in him feelings of loneliness and abandonment. Over the years J. began to understand that he could not trust anyone, in fact, he did not socialize anymore. Slowly, detachment from society was the only way to escape pain, thus continuing to be invisible. He said he had never dated a girl before; he was completely closed in on himself. He went to live alone at the age of 20 and became a nurse.   When he was twenty-one years old, he began to feel constantly sad and downed, so much so that he thought several times that he would end his life. When J. was about twenty-eight years old, the feelings of uselessness and inadequacy that   pervaded   him, for   a long time now, caused him many difficulties. These negative feelings were definitely taking hold of him. The patient began to experience intense and painful emotions for which he could not find an explanation. J. didn't have any friends, he didn't trust anyone, so he started to abuse heroin. The patient was able to get the substance from his work. For J. the dose of heroin became necessary, it "self-treated" the painful emotions that pervaded him. Initially he took substances sporadically but soon realized that the drug was a trusted friend, the fundamental figure he had never had in life. J. tried outpatient therapies for a few sessions, hoping to stop the heroin abuse, but   the   therapies   failed.   In the next two years she continued to use heroin to feel better and became addicted using it every day. His foreman noticed irregularities in the dressing of patients at that time and some medications had been missing for some time. J was accused of stealing his meds. He was suspended from his work and undertook three months of outpatient treatment to alleviate his addiction. Unfortunately, the treatment failed and continued to take drugs. Then he went into a three-month residential program, but they asked him to leave because he was creating problems. Over time he decided to be more cooperative with the program and agreed to follow a treatment to be readmitted to the residential program. After completing the program, he was discharged. After his resignation, he was "clean" for five and a half months. J. was really frightened by his resignation and by the interruption of the therapy because, far from the assistance and the therapeutic control, the temptations to use the medicines, when he saw them at work or   when   he felt negative   emotions, were   very   intense.   He specified that he wanted to be honest in his EMDR treatment because   he realized that continued substance abuse would jeopardize his future. The evaluation of J.'s medical history indicates unresolved traumas, traumatic memories that are the cause of the disorder. The patient's contempt for his parents and himself was linked to the numerous physical and psychological abuses that J. had experienced, as a result, the patient, directed to any person the distrust and resentment felt. This formed the basis of   his   relationship   problems.   As   an   optimal   goal, psychotherapists specializing in EMDR will work on these traumatic memories to enable J. to adopt functional and positive behaviors towards himself and others.

EMDR on its legal situation

J. decided to rely on EMDR when he was overwhelmed by fear and fear of taking substances or drugs again. He reported that one day he was called home by a person who was investigating the thefts in the hospital where J. was working, and the guy accused him of being a thief. After that phone call, the patient had a great deal of fear and anxiety about losing his job and his license to work as a nurse. The target chosen for the negative cognition was "my boss persecutes me; he thinks I'm a thief". This conviction about himself was linked to what had been passed on to him   all his life until then, namely, "I am bad, I am an outcast, I am useless". On a continuum of 0 to 10 of the Subjective Units of Disturbance (SOUTH) scales, J.'s anxiety was 10. The positive conviction I wanted was "I was sick, I couldn't do anything else to overcome the situation".   The Validity of Cognition (VOC) on a scale of 1 to 7, was at level 2. During the sessions with the EMDR J. became able to recognize the feelings that drove him to suicide and the desire to run and hide in the house without doing anything. J. noticed that EMDR made it easier for him to recognize wrong emotions and beliefs about himself, he was relieved of the feelings of being "bad and worthless" transmitted to him by his family when he criticized him or accused him of alleged transgressions. After the initial treatment, future-oriented positive models were installed to help him cope with current situations. These include contacting a lawyer   who

73

could defend him from the accusations of theft made against him. During the treatment phase on the current situation, the level of the SOUTH dropped from 10 to 2, as he felt ready to face the charges that involved him. His VOC score for positive cognition reached 5 at the end of the session. J. felt quite confident that he could get legal assistance and then dealt with his situation. The patient stated that after the EMDR session he managed to overcome the situation satisfactorily and that he did not have the suicidal ideas or the impulses to consume drugs that he often did. In fact, in a month, J.'s judicial situation was completely resolved. His license was not revoked because the evidence was insufficient. Any charges brought against J., so it was filed. The EMDR treatment has been very effective in reprocessing dysfunctional knowledge, leading J. to address the culpable situation in which he was involved and, at the same time, in preventing relapses. J. improved his insight after the first EMDR session, as he realized how past trauma, experienced at a young age, was connected to the present, immobilizing it, making it relive emotions of discouragement and uselessness.

EMDR on the issues raised with its sponsor

As time and EMDR sessions progressed, more material emerged from J. The therapy helped him to realize that his low self-esteem was rooted in the past dysfunctional model that had been passed on to him, which caused him to feel like he was useless, unhappy and victim in the present. At one sitting, J. arrived in a state of extreme agitation and anxiety, while exposing what had happened to him was overwhelmed by feelings of sadness and betrayal. He admitted that he had taken painkillers for a herniated disc and that his sponsor (a former drug addict who acts as a support during craving for those still taking substances) accused him of not respecting abstinence and having had a relapse. When the problem was examined, it became apparent that J. did not tell his doctor about his substance addiction and was therefore prescribed a pain medication containing an opioid. J. however, had taken it as prescribed, so without abusing it. The patient recognized that he had made a mistake when he could not ask if the prescribed drug contained substances "familiar" to him. J. had well understood his problem, but felt that it was an "honest, acceptable mistake" and that his sponsor could give him the benefit of the doubt.

J. agreed to deal with the situation and thanks to the EMDR treated the adverse feelings arising from such an event. Th e target chosen for the negative conviction was: "my sponsor betrayed me". The negative cognition included: "I've been bad, I'm a hypocrite, I hate myself, I'm not worthy to live". The SOUTH for anxiety was 10. Positive cognitions, on the other hand, included: "I am worthy of living, this is the point of view of my sponsor, I can handle the situation". J. said that when confronted with his sponsor, he relived the way his father had always treated him and how he felt, again, rejected. He has been able to elaborate a series of memories, corresponding to early childhood, closely related to the current situation. J. recognized that his first impulse was to run and hide in his room, just as he did as a child. The re-elaboration of the traumas helped J. to identify these situations as past, and therefore finished. Subsequently, the patient was able to recognize that his sponsor had an all too harsh perception of him and that he should have told him how he felt because of the unpleasant situation. The installation of a future functional behavioral model consisted in the fact that J. did his best to try to maintain sobriety and abstinence, and that he should live the mistake he made as a teaching. From that experience on, J. would always ask his doctor for drugs that would not stimulate addiction. The patient was prepared to tolerate painful feelings, even if his sponsor refused to work with him again, for example because he did not accept the situation. At the end of the EMDR session, J.'s SOUTH level decreased to 2.5. His VOC score was 5, which was considered acceptable as he would only feel really good about himself after talking to his sponsor. In this situation, too, EMDR proved to be fundamental. The method allowed J. to deal with the difficult situation and to solve the problem effectively. In addition, EMDR allowed him to tolerate the levels of negative emotion that arose when his sponsor decided that he could no longer work with him. J. was able to accept his sponsor 's point of view and decided that he would need to find someone else who was more tolerant.

EMDR on temptations and likely spill-over effects

J. continued to feel a strong desire to use drugs, caused by the bottles of drugs he saw in his work environment. He reported that one of his roommates was recently on pain medication and J. was very tempted by this situation. He admitted that when he went to visit his parents, he was struggling to give in or not to the temptation to take medication present in the locker where they were stored. His temptations to take drugs, when they were within his reach, corresponded to the target for four EMDR sessions, until J. felt more confident and able to resist temptation and remain so sober. Targets included emotions and physical sensations associated with the temptation to use medication. J.'s negative knowledge was, "I'm vulnerable, I can't do it without the drugs."   His SOUTH level was 8.5. As for the positive cognitions, the patient stated: "I manage my drug-free life, I can manage my feelings, I can manage the situation properly". His VOC score was 3 at the start of the session. At the end of the four sessions his SOUTH level dropped   to 2 and his VOC score increased to 7. During the repeated processing of such targets, it was possible to access many beliefs and feelings about his future recovery. J. was able to recognize that he felt the need to take drugs to feel good and that he did not want to deal with the pain of people in the past, what he most feared was to deal with difficult situations. The patient recognized that he was not used to receiving attention and care from others and therefore perceived himself as "crazy", for this reason he wanted to keep his psychotherapy secret. In addition, J. initially confessed that he hoped to be able to manage his life by occasionally using drugs and that he would suffer without them. During subsequent sessions, he was able to admit that drugs had made his life unmanageable   and that he could not use them in a controlled manner. J. was able to recognize   that if he took even one pill, he would never stop. He also managed to communicate positive cognitions, such as imagining himself as an honest and active member of the group therapy program for anonymous narcotics, completing the 12 characteristic steps of the therapy, and thus overcoming his fear of life. J. However, he was still reluctant to use EMDR to resolve the first traumatic memories in a more comprehensive way. The installations consisted of preparing for future triggers of relapse and increasing self-confidence, i.e. feeling able to handle adverse situations without falling back into drug addiction. In particular, J. said that when he was in the company of his sponsor and other close friends, he often felt the overwhelming desire to use drugs, but to escape this prevailing desire he chose to move away from the group.

EMDR on the likely harassment at 14 years of age

During the course of the therapy, J. stated that the EMDR sessions were extremely useful in curbing his desire to take the drug and this was important because he implemented in J. his coping skills. Whenever very painful feelings, such as abandonment, and low self-esteem, were reactivated, J. would have liked to cloud them. However, thanks to his rediscovered insight skills and recognition   of his dysfunctional   response model, J.   was   able to   identify his vulnerability and thus better prepare himself in the management of his negative emotions. J. was willing to undergo the targeting session, to solve this problem of entirely family origin (because of the recurrent pressure), while remaining vulnerable to relapses. Another difficult issue to solve, after a year of treatment with EMDR, emerged following a crisis of J. During the EMDR sessions, J. reported a memory void corresponding to the period of his adolescence. As his recovery progressed, a memory of harassment emerged. The re-elaboration of the memory favored the appearance of further previous memories. J. reported that while he was sleeping one afternoon, when he woke up, he was molested by his uncle. The patient was about 14 years old. This memory was perceived by J. in a very disturbing way.

He said that he began to take drugs because the sensations that overwhelmed him were too painful and oppressive. The hypothesis of the doctors was that probably   the harassment could never actually have happened, because in many years of therapy (without EMDR) never emerged what reported by J. However, no matter how well-founded they were, it was clinically important to process these emotionally charged images so that we could deal with the anguish we felt and the possible influence on current dysfunctional behavior. EMDR was used to help J.   manage   the   pain caused   by the image   of   harassment.   The SOUTH level of anxiety was   10.   His negative   cognitions were, "I'm vulnerable, I'm a victim." His positive knowledge was   "it's over, what happened to me belongs to the past". J. underwent   two sessions of EMDR aimed at solving the problem completely. This became evident in the SOUTH level which equaled 2, as J. felt he could handle the situation. During g the EMDR, J.   elaborated   the image   of the   harassment   as well   as   his   feelings   of   anger, victimization, abandonment   and   more of his inability to talk to someone than had happened to him in the past.

The installations were aimed at future coping, including asking for support and support from his sponsor, his family, and other friends. In addition, J. was prepared to meet with the alleged   perpetrator   of the harassment, when   he would   feel   more   secure. The patient decided that he would like to interact with him in a superficial way, without digging too much into the past. J. felt much more capable of dealing with any event in his life, in fact, thanks to EMDR and, above all, to his great willpower, he was able to meet, without excessive anxiety, the "alleged" perpetrator of harassment during a family reunion. For J., EMDR was extremely helpful   in accelerating recovery and preventing relapse.

J.'s treatment program is specifically aimed at individuals recovering from addiction to psychoactive substances. EMDR was used intermittently whenever J.'s feelings became unbearable. The treatment gave him the opportunity to neutralize underlying traumatic memories. Through EMDR, the patient's insight increased and with it the rapid acquisition of new, much more functional behaviors. The underlying traumatic material has been transformed little by little, this was every time J. proved to be more able to integrate previous experiences. J. was able to stay sober and did paid work for about eighteen months since he began his therapy. EMDR has been very useful in strengthening J.'s recovery programmed and has also reduced the likelihood of relapse, neutralizing the underlying risk factors and traumatic memories, by installing an appropriate future-oriented action model.

STUDIES CARRIED OUT IN ITALY

Some studies in Italy provide preliminary information on the method and the purpose of the research, justifying them also on the fact that, thanks to their adherence to the treatment, it will be possible to evaluate and demonstrate the effectiveness or otherwise of EMDR in the treatment of drug addicts, compared to other methods, underlining that this is a procedure already validated for other issues, for at least fifteen years. Finally, the practitioner will advise the patient concerned to make an appointment with the expert who will better explain what the program consists of. If the patient is not satisfied with the interview, he or she can still be redirected to another treatment course. The information sheet on EMDR and informed consent on EMDR and research objectives will be provided. The research is divided into phases, which start, as just indicated by the reception, and end with the follow-up at 3, 6 and 12 months.

Phase 1: the subjects arrive at the reception where an operator of the structure will welcome the user's request. At this stage the subject will be informed about the available programmers and EMDR research. It will be sent to the doctor for routine examinations and if not interested in the EMDR protocol, it will be included in the standard care pathways of the Sir.

Phase 2: Subjects participating in the program will be tested and sent for interview with the EMDR therapist who will give all the information on the protocol. This is how the experimental phase will begin, in which the subjects will be involved in 18 EMDR sessions. The subjects of the control group, once they have completed the tests and had an interview with a doctor, will follow the routine program of the public structure.

Phase 3: after the experimental phase, after six months, the subjects of the experimental group will be submitted again to the tests and to the interview with the doctor. The same applies to the control group which, six months after the start of the program me, will be tested and interviewed by the doctor.

Phase 4: follow-up at 6 and 12 months for both groups.

The research carried out by the team of EMDR psychotherapists, in summary, aims to assess:

1. The effectiveness of EMDR in reducing compulsive behavior to the use of substances also in relation to the shorter time taken to achieve the objectives compared to the standard protocols;

2. Increasing compliance with treatment with an EMDR protocol;

3. The effectiveness of the method in reducing the emotional impact of traumatic events of the abuser patient.

The evaluation of the reduction of compulsive behavior will be done through the analysis of drug tests for research purposes will be processed the data of beginning, middle and end of treatment and, the self-assessment scale SCQ-39. Treatment compliance will be assessed by analyzing the subjects who remain in therapy and who end the program. While the effectiveness of the EMDR method in reducing the emotional impact of stressful events is assessed by comparing the results of the BDI, STAI, and INVENTORY tests.

STRESSFUL ANDUMATIC EVENTS OF LIFE

The administration of the EMDR protocol consists of 18 sessions, for a period of treatment of about 6 months. The aim is to be able to administer the protocol to about 30 subjects diagnosed with alcohol, cocaine, heroin or polyassumption addiction. The treatment of patients follows specific steps:

1) Establishing a positive therapeutic relationship

2) Gather information about past or present traumas and addiction history

3) Strengthen motivation for treatment through positive and achievable therapeutic goals and enhance personal resources

4) Desensitization of traumatic events in chronological order

5) Desensitization of "first time" memory and addiction triggering factor(s)

6) Desensitization of the level of compulsion "level of urgency" and of the trigger's "triggers" the addictive behavior

7) Desensitization of the memory of relapses

8) Installation of a positive IO status for each triggering factor

The tests used are:

- BDI (Beck Depression Inventory Scale) for the detection of the risk of depression and to discriminate patients with clinical depression compared to non-depressed psychiatric patients.

- DES (Dissociative Experiences Scale by E.B. Bernstein and F.W. Putnam) for measuring the level and type of dissociative experience

INVENTORY OF STRESSFUL AND TRAUMATIC EVENTS IN LIFE

- STAI (STAI-Y: State-Trait Anxiety Inventory - form Y): Self-assessment questionnaire for trait and state anxiety

SCQ-39

Since the research is still ongoing, the analysis of test data is still in the process of being processed, but it is nevertheless interesting to dwell on some clinical cases to give relevance to the way in which the EMDR is used.

The clinical case of A.
A. has completed 15 meetings to date, 11 of which with EMDR. Male patient is 32 years old and appears to be a polyassumption. The first contact with the drug services took place in 2005. He never wanted to follow a psychotherapeutic treatment, but only sporadic interviews with psychologists and the psychiatrist.

Over the years he has occasionally attended the SerD, following the drug therapy for a few months and then disappearing for as many months. In the past he was treated with Buprefene and now Naloxone. A. presents himself as a very shy person, smiling, little cared for. He accepts to be part of the experimental group and seems to be very motivated after having had explanations about the protocol. The patient has always respected the appointments and the two times that, due to work problems, he could not attend the sessions, he informed the psychotherapist in a timely manner. A. has repeatedly tried to combat substance addiction, but his inability to insight has made every attempt to fail.

History

A. has a degree and is employed by a company. She has an older sister, married and with children. Daddy's been dead recently. He describes his family as quiet, with good relations between its members. No situations of economic distress or traumatic events emerge from the interview. A. seems to have had a happy childhood. He tells of his adolescence and adulthood, underlining some relational problems especially with girls because of his shyness, but tends to describe the period as quiet, without traumatic events. He always went to school well with the exception of the fourth year, where it is rejected because of the numerous absences. Privately A. recovers the year and then goes back to study at a public high school, where he graduates with excellent grades. The patient describes himself as very capable in study and work but with little memory of the events that make him feel bad. A. says: "I say that I have been well, but, perhaps, if I am here today, I am not so well, but I do not know what I have. I tend to forget the things that make me sick." The first contact with the substances, in fact, takes place very early: at 14 years THC, at 15 years amphetamine and ecstasy, at 16 years cocaine and at 18 years heroine by inhalation. The family is not aware of A.'s problem, he will communicate it to his mother and sister, after the death of his father. The patient explains his initiation into substances by saying that his friends used and used them, and his curiosity led him to try them and then become addicted to them. A. says that his problem is that he is a "curious" and "presumptuous" person, such thoughts lead him to the false belief that he can stop at any time. The patient makes the beginning of his addiction story coincide with the time he started buying heroin, i.e. at the age of 18. From that moment on, the use of the substance was no longer r sporadic. The idea that emerges during a session is that he needs heroin to calm himself down: "If I have such an idea, I must have been very agitated". The patient is still convinced that the drug is needed to calm down and fall asleep. He describes how good his relationship with colleagues and friends is. He lives alone and on weekends he returns to the country where his mother lives. At the time of taking charge, the patient tested positive for heroin and cocaine. The objective on which A. would like to work is: "Remove the fixed nail of the drug". This would allow him to have better relationships and give priority to friendships not related to the drug world and maybe even have a relationship. As a safe place A. uses the image of a tropical island and the feeling of relaxation, tranquility and security that he feels when imagining lying on the beach in the sun. The key word will be "PARADISE". Tenacity and constancy were the resources that emerged in A. when he was determined to pursue a goal, they were identified by the therapist when the patient spoke about his school and university career. The resulting feeling of strength, i.e. strength as a positive state of the ego, was installed by the therapist through bilateral movements and subsequently fixed. A. promptly used his safe place at home,

specially to fall asleep to the point that, after the first three interviews, he said he no longer used heroin to fall asleep. Now the use is limited to consumption with friends. It remains difficult for the therapist to find traumatic events to work with the EMDR on, as A. claims that she has not experienced them or has no memory of them. The only two events reported are: the death of his father and the rejection of the fourth year, the oldest and most disturbing event. Such events do not seem to be directly linked to the history of addiction, since they occur after its inception. The difficulty in tracing disturbing events seems to be linked to dissociative defenses, as, in fact, will emerge later during EMDR sessions. The drug in its use, seems to be linked to its placatory aspect the emotional activation of the patient, modulator of shyness and therefore means facilitating social relations.

EMDR *on the most disturbing traumatic event*

The administration of EMDR on the most disturbing traumatic episode for the patient is recorded by the therapist as follows in its most significant parts. The most painful image for A. was to see the pictures that reported the non-admission to the state exams. The negative conviction (CN) was "I have no control/I can't do anything anymore", the positive conviction (CP) was "I can do something", the VOC level corresponded to 1 and the SOUTH to 9, the associated emotion was the anger and localization of the emotional discomfort in the chest. A. showed considerable difficulty in the EMDR session, he said he felt his head was empty, he didn't remember, he didn't have any images or words. The derealization that A. had for a few seconds was perceived by the patient, who was very concerned about it. The therapist then interrupted the EMDR session and decided to take advantage of the image and emotion associated with the safe place to decrease concern and anxiety. In the next session the psychotherapist asked to recover the image from which they had started the previous time and A. described it as distant, blurred and no longer disturbing: the level of the SOUTH corresponded to 2. The patient is unbelieving that the image is no longer disturbing and therefore cannot go down to zero in the SOUTH, so the therapist accepts this value as ecological. The CP stated was: "it's not an important thing, I became an engineer, I can do something". The VOC increased to 6 and then 7 after installation.

EMDR *on the trauma associated with daddy's death.*

A.'s disturbing image was seeing his dad in a coma on his hospital bed. It was not possible for the psychotherapist to trace the Negative Conviction. A. appeared to be completely blocked. The SOUTH level was 10 and the associated emotion was sadness. The therapist continued, however, with the desensitization without CN but A. at that time felt headaches, feelings of cold that penetrated him. The elaboration seemed not to proceed. The therapist, at this point, decided to tell A. that she might not even verbalize what she was feeling, and told her to warn her when she would feel more comfortable or when she would display positive images. The EMDR session continued with desensitization until the patient was relaxed again. At the next meeting the therapist asked to recover the image from which they started the previous session , and also this time the level of the SOUTH was 2 but not zero because even here, for the patient it was not possible to believe that such an event was no longer disturbing. The therapist therefore decided not to perform the installation, since A. did not report either CP or CN. The session continued with an integrated cognitive intervention borrowing the processing of the next time. The loss of a parent and all the related emotions represent something that cannot be modified, but it could be given a different meaning. This cognitive strategy proved effective for A. when the therapist intervened on the memory of the rejection, in fact the meaning associated with the event changed from "I have no control, I cannot do anything" to "no longer important because I can do something, today I am engineer", so if you change the meaning, the disorder can decrease.

A. appeared happy and reassured. After a few sessions with EMDR, drug use began to become more sporadic.

EMDR on the history of addiction

Compared to the history of addiction, A. pointed out that the most disturbing event was drug use after a fight with a friend and, in order to relieve his anger and nervousness, he went to the sea alone. The disturbing image associated with this event was: "I'm swimming in the sea, it's very hot outside". What the patient considered most unpleasant was a feeling of cold that invaded him. The C.N. corresponded to A. a: "I'm weak." From this statement the therapist continued with the survey of the C.P. or "I can be strong". With a VOC scale value of 2, and with a SUD 10, whose corresponding emotion was embarrassment, with a full-body localization. In front of A., on the table, there was the drug therapy used by him and the patient claimed that his weakness was related to addiction to drugs. The therapy continued with an integrated cognitive intervention, underlining that asking for help is a sign of strength and that A. was proving to be very strong and tenacious in going to the SerD, in continuing the very difficult and demanding meetings. Afterwards the therapist decided to install the C.P. "I can be strong", to which the patient attributed a value of 7 in the VOC. In that period, despite the difficulties in carrying out complete sessions of EMDR, where episodes of derealization continued, it seemed that the process of elaboration between one session and the next progressed positively.

A. was very enthusiastic about the work and results he was achieving with the therapist. In fact, the urine test came back negative. The protocol continued with the elaboration of the worst event and the last episode linked to the history of addiction and then with the desensitization of the factors triggering the compulsion starting from the triggers with a lower LOU (level of urgency). The more times the emotion will be embarrassment and the feeling of confusion and headache, even if the patient will be less afraid of it. The intensity of the compulsion linked to the various events fell to 0 except for the most intense event which remained at 1. It is related to the feeling of unstoppable desire to take the drug at the sight of someone who smokes heroin.

A. says he doesn't know if in the future he can be sure to resist this temptation. In fact, this event will take place two weeks after the sitting. A. will claim that he was unable to say no to friends who offered him to smoke. The protocol continues with the desensitization of relapses and with the establishment of a future scenario where the patient will later be able to move away from the group of friends at the time of drug use or completely change round of friendships. The urine test was negative for heroin and positive for cocaine.

A. said that he had smoked a cigarette soaked in cocaine and that for him this substance is not a problem, he doesn't look for it, he doesn't buy it, but he happens to use it when his "friends" offer it to him? Cocaine wasn't a staple. The therapist and the patient agreed together that in order to assume a future drug trial, the urine tests should also be negative for cocaine. In the following sessions A. underwent the urine tests from which he was negative for both drugs.

The patient also managed to manage the future scenario in a quiet and safe way, functional modes adopted in psychotherapy sessions with EMDR.

A. said that when friends decided to smoke heroin, he chose to leave the group. The patient showed that he was really satisfied and proud of himself, because he reached the goal he had set himself; heroin was no longer a recurring and predominant thought, on the contrary he was surprised that they spent whole days without having thought at all about drugs. In addition, the patient is beginning to remember very ancient past events such as an accident at the age of five years. The therapy is currently in its final stage.

The clinical case of B.
B. to date has held 17 meetings, 14 of which with EMDR. 37-year-old female patient. Currently taking heroin for injection. The first contact with the drug services took place in 1996. B. is remarkably robust, she was diagnosed with depression, and for this reason she is being treated with antidepressants. The level of education corresponds to the third grade, unemployed and living with her partner, who is also in care at the addiction services. B. made two attempts at dissection at the age of 19 at the sleep clinic, but after a few months he had a relapse. At the age of 22 he went to a clinic to detoxify and managed to stay absent for a long time. B. said during the interview that he had suffered from epilepsy, so the psychotherapist EMDR will proceed in desensitization only with tapping. At the beginning of the treatment, the patient will tend to skip appointments without warning, justifying not having woken up. During the course of therapy B. will gradually be more correct and attentive to schedules and meetings, and when he cannot go to the appointments will notify in advance, still allowing the therapy to proceed albeit with longer times but basically preventing a drop-out.

B. showed up at the first appointment with little care, dressed in black and with a low expressiveness of facial expression. She said she had recurrent panic attacks and widespread anxiety that prevented her from doing anything. The patient claimed to have no friendships, had no job, and spent her time at home alone caring for her many cats.

History

B. was adopted at one year of age, her biological mother had no Italian origins.   The story of the adoption was ambiguous because B. told of a lady who treated her for a few years and then was finally adopted by those who were her future parents. The relationship with the adoptive parents was described by the patient as conflictual, the father as severe and challenging and the mother concentrated on caring for her natural brother older than a few years. B. tells of his epileptic crises that were mixed with memories of   visions   and   contacts   with   his   natural   mother and with   Our Lady.   For this reason, the patient talks about the continuous psychiatric examinations, visits by exorcists and psychics all more or less between the ages of 8 and 10 years of age. The first contact   with the substances took place very early: at 13 he started smoking tobacco, at 14 years THC, alcohol and super alcohol, at 16 years cocaine and ecstasy, at 18 years heroin. In the inventory of Giannantonio's stressful events, two rapes were reported: one at the age of 14 and one in a group at 18. The patient learned of the death of the biological mother by reading a newspaper article about the discovery of a woman's body.   The details described in the article gave the patient the impression that it was her mother. Even today, the patient is still keeping the above article. B. told of how he prostituted himself to buy drugs. During the interviews he tells of other episodes of abuse, the first of which occurred at the age of 8 years by a doctor, during a visit. B. claimed that he had always had difficulties in social relations because of his "oddities".

The patient's sentimental stories were always linked to stories with boys and men who were addicted to drugs.

The goal on which B. would like to work was to "find some energy to get back to painting and look for a job". This would have allowed her to be more positive and to recover some self-esteem. Following the EMDR protocol, the patient uses the image of a   beach   at   sunset as a safe place. This image was often used at home during the early days of therapy and seemed to have a very positive effect on anxiety, as it gave B. a feeling of immediate well-being. The positive resources of the patient were found in her creativity, in her ability to match colors and in her ability to make order.   For B., the state of well-being, positivity and self-satisfaction   he   felt   after   creating a picture was fundamental to the therapy.   These positive feelings will represent the positive state of the ego and will be installed through the tapping and then anchored.

EMDR on the most disturbing traumatic event

B. declared that the most disturbing and oldest event was linked to the "abandonment" of the biological mother. The patient remembers a very small image of herself in the standing couch resting on the bars. This memory is associated with the image of the mother preparing something to eat, while around the very small patient there were many men playing basketball over her head. The negative conviction (C.N.) found was: "I'm not worth anything". The patient said, "I'm not loved, Mom doesn't care about me." The therapist wanted to get to the bottom of this belief in order to give the patient insight. B. later stated: "I'm strange, I have something wrong, I'm not worth anything". The positive conviction that emerged was (C.P.): "I am a valid person". The validity of the positive conviction (VOC) was 1 and the emotion experienced was sadness. SOUTH level was 10.   The location of the disorder was the heart. The treatment with EMDR continued with the desensitization for the above-mentioned event, and this happened for some sessions. This gave access to another important channel, namely the focusing of the image of the mother preparing the food. B. claimed that the mother was taking care of her with what little she had. The patient, with the support of the therapist, came to the conclusion that the adoption was an act of care, and not of abandonment because B.'s mother had no choice but to separate herself from her so as to hope for a better life for her daughter. From this memory, the patient was able to begin to recover themes of care. The channel that opened here was that of the feeling of guilt for the anger felt towards the biological mother and for not being up to the hard price that the mother had to pay, in other words: depriving herself of her daughter in exchange for a better life for her. The C.N. that B. reported was "I was wrong." The traumatic events that followed the adoption were many, such as having sex for money, or having invented that her brother had abused her, or even the violence suffered at the age of eighteen. The therapy continued with the elaboration of these events and in particular   the violence at eighteen years of age of which B. had a precise image that often came to   his   mind   as   a   flashback k or,   the   patient in a machine,   stunned by the effect of drugs that is thrown on the ground in the middle of the mud "Like a rejection". Subsequently, the therapist worked on the alleged violence by her non-biological older brother, who said that the patient had suffered but that in reality it never happened.   The   CP   installed   was "I   learned   from   this".   Thanks to the EMDR therapy, the patient reported to a SerD doctor that he was better off: "not being able to understand the goddess of how certain disturbing images until then had lost their anxiogenic characteristic after the EMDR sessions".   In the   meantime, the   patient resumed   painting   and   taking   care   of the   house.   The desensitization of traumatic events continued with another cluster of C.N. related events: "I am weak". These were mainly related to the bond with the adoptive father. The C.P. installed was "I'm strong" which will allow B. to begin to devote himself to the care of himself, to the markets of craftsmanship to sell his creations of jewelry.

EMDR on the history of addiction

B. made her beginning of her addiction coincide with her first cigarette, at the age of thirteen, and with the challenge that her adoptive father threw at her: "if you smoke you have to do it before me". So it was that B. will read this event as a lack of love, attention and protection of his father towards him. The patient, in fact, said: "the stakes will have to be higher and higher to require attention and care.

Desensitization of triggering factors

The patient continued to use drugs, albeit sporadically (once a month). This consumption was related to the attendance of a place with the companion where they went from time to time. The desensitization of the compulsive factors (LOU) related to the time of drug use failed to reach but stopped at 3. In the next session the patient claimed to have been to the place where she often went to consume drugs and had used them. He said that he had thought a lot about the session while he was there, he felt the need to leave that place, and that from one moment to the next he would get up and give up consuming heroin.   That was not the case. The patient said she didn't want to give up "that ritual and pact with her partner". B. did not see the danger because in his daily life the drug was no longer part of it. So, the therapist decided not to proceed with the desensitization of the events triggering the compulsion and focused on the future scenario on which B. wants to work. She will choose active engagement in seeking work, which allowed the patient/therapist couple to focus on the blockage caused by the feeling of inadequacy for certain work roles, such as being a saleswoman, because they know they do not look good. Through EMDR, the positive resources of the patient were strengthened and anchored in the future scenario. In the next session, the patient told the therapist that she had gone around her city, with the aim of delivering her resume to the shops. In addition, the patient claimed to have plans to sell his creations in various markets, thanks to an acquaintance with whom he will also begin a friendship. B. to date is well-kept, well-dressed and smiling. Drug therapy continues and she seems very motivated to stop taking drugs. Currently, EMDR therapy is still ongoing.

CONCLUSIONS IN STUDY CASE

With this thesis work we wanted to demonstrate how EMDR (Eye Movement Desensitization and Reprocessing - Desensitization and Re-elaboration through Eye Movements) can be an adequate treatment for abusers or drug addicts because, this method, considered evidence-based, is a powerful tool for a better adaptive condition even in subjects difficult to treat such as drug addicts. In recent years there have been more studies and scientific research on EMDR than any other method used for the treatment of trauma and traumatic memories. The results of this work have shown how this therapeutic approach can open a new dimension in psychotherapy. Since 1989 Francine Shapiro has been spreading her precious discoveries all over the world. EMDR is a complex method that requires adequate and comprehensive training, appropriate use of procedures and deep interaction between clinician, method and patient (Dworkin, 2010). Becoming psychotherapists specialized in EMDR treatment consists in having a "key" that allows patients to access their memories born from traumatic experiences related to the past, they manifest themselves in the present through behaviors dysfunctional and difficult to manage. On the other hand, for the psychotherapist, EMDR offers an innovative way of understanding and intervening on the pathology. Thanks to the exposure of some clinical cases, it has been possible to prove the effectiveness of EMDR and how much the improvement is evident in the daily lives of patients. The EMDR protocol consists of 8 steps: 1. patient history; 2. patient preparation; 3. assessment; 4. desensitization; 5. installation; 6. body scan; 7. Closure; 8. Reassessment. Each phase is fundamental, during the psychotherapeutic sessions you cannot omit any of them, you must pay close attention to the anamnestic phase. The history of the patient, the events apparently "forgotten" thanks to the desensitization return accessible. Desensitization and reconsolidation, which can be observed during an EMDR session, show how in the elaboration of the memory of the traumatic experience one can observe the patient who can perceive the memory far, far, while he incorporates the emotions appropriate to the situation and eliminates the disturbing physical sensations.

In short, through EMDR a dysfunctional memory becomes more functional, which will allow the patient to recover an adaptive condition better than the traumatic experience. The integration in amnesty networks, allows the traumatic memory to no longer represent a limit but, integrating into memory in a functional and adaptive way, will allow the patient to proceed with his life. After the elaboration process, patients remember the traumatic event but feel it belongs to the past, removing the emotionally disturbing effects that this experience had produced. It is surprising how resolutive the right/left eye movements or the tapping (drumming) really are, in the rapid desensitization of traumatic memories. The result is a real cognitive restructuring that significantly reduces the patient's symptoms such as emotional stress, intrusive thoughts, anxiety, flashbacks, nightmares. The EMDR, integrated with any psychotherapeutic, cognitive-behavioral and other approach, was initially addressed to the treatment of Post-Traumatic Stress Disorder, is currently a widely used method also for the treatment of various pathologies and psychological disorders, in this regard M. Balbo (2006), proposes a vision of EMDR as "an integral approach among psychotherapies", confirming how theoretical concepts, expressed by scholars belonging to different clinical orientations, protocol and intervention procedures are adaptable to the main and contemporary schools of thought of the Universe of psychotherapeutic approaches. The EMDR is based on the model of Adaptive Information Processing which presupposes the existence of a system of self-healing within the person, capable of processing the information until the balance of the system is reached that is in a state of imbalance, following a traumatic event or strong stress. The pathology is considered as the preservation of a disturbing memory in its original form, that is, including all the emotional load of that given moment. Complex stress situations generally arise in the context of interpersonal relationships, where "traumatic" events combine with a failure and serious disturbances of the primary care system and are all the more important the more they invest the subject in the phase of personality formation. Such situations seem to predict, at a later age, behaviors of drug abuse, vagrancy, prolonged inactivity etc. Hase (2004) shows that 75% of Vietnam War veterans had alcohol addiction problems. The author points out that patients with PTSD show significantly more problems of drug dependence than other patients (21-43 % vs 8-24 %) while Mills et al. (2005) in a study of 459 subjects treated for opioid use confirms that 42% have comorbidities with a post-traumatic stress disorder. The studies of Zwebwn and Yeary et al. (2006) and Cox (2007), show the comorbidity of dependence with the presence of traumas, even small ones, which if not solved can still cause a major disorder. Even Joe E's work. Thornton, (2003) highlight the comorbidity between alcohol dependence and PTSD by reporting that patients with PTSD have a lifetime alcohol dependence 2/3 times greater than the general population, while adolescents hospitalized for alcohol are 5 times more likely to receive a co-diagnosis for post-traumatic stress disorder. Donald (2009) points out the high comorbidity between PTSD and SOUTH (Substance Use Disorder), pointing out that generally people with addictions are actually treated only for such behavior and rarely receive treatment for PTSD. In addition, neuropsychological studies suggest that trauma and stress can produce changes in the brain putting the subject at risk for future substance addiction behaviors. These hypotheses are now confirmed by the use of new instruments that allow to analyze the brain not only in its structure, but also in its mode of operation. The above-mentioned studies have made a fundamental contribution in assessing the correlations between substance use and brain areas, showing how these change more or less permanently when they are affected by exogenous chemicals. In this sense, investigations conducted with functional magnetic resonance imaging have demonstrated the relationship between cocaine craving and stress, as reported by Duncan (2007) and how the subject's reaction to stressful events can act as a predictor of his vulnerability to addiction. Functional imaging studies using single photon emission tomography (SPECT) and positron emission tomography (PET) have shown significant changes in brain flow in patients with PTSD during the review of trauma. Increases and decreases in flow have been reported in the hippocampus, amygdala, medial prefrontal cortex, anterior and posterior cingulate, and temporal cortex. The prevailing model links the symptoms of PTSD to a lack of inhibition of the amygdala, hyperactivated by the sensation of impending threat, by the prefrontal cortex. It has also been proposed that structural changes in the hippocampus and anterior cingulate revealed by structural magnetic resonance imaging (MRI) are caused by neuronal response to stress. The objective of EMDR, in such situations and in the same way in other psychopathologies, is to act on the cortex temporo-parieto-occipital, convolved in PTSD, and the value of neuroimaging is fundamental both in revealing the neurobiological effects of EMDR and in determining the value of structural investigations in predicting its effectiveness. In the first part of the thesis, the above has been highlighted, but in order to define the correlation between abuse or dependence on psychoactive substances and post-traumatic stress disorder, the different categories of drug addiction have been widely illustrated. Lewin (1928) divides drug addiction into different categories, each category describing the drug substance you belong to it. Abstinence crisis, craving, drug- seeking behavior, dysfunctional behaviors and unmanageable desires are present in each of the 3 clinical cases exposed in the thesis work. Thanks to the numerous researches carried out all over the world, such as the research carried out by Shapiro F., Vogelmann-Sine, S., & Sine, L. (1994), the efficacy of EMDR in the treatment of drug addicts has proved possible. Fundamental will be the research, still ongoing, carried out in Italy by some highly trained EMDR psychotherapists at a SerD in Lazio. Dr. S. Zaccari, Dr. M. Simone and Dr. A. Di Leo, with the efficient collaboration of the operators of the public facility, have demonstrated how, for some patients, the EMDR method is valid and rapidly resolving in the treatment of PTSD related to substance abuse and addiction. This has been proven during the treatment phases. Patients initially showed considerable difficulty in accepting and pursuing the EMDR protocol adapted to substance dependence, absent themselves and not respecting timetables. Soon, with the succession of sessions, their collaborative side and the strong desire to overcome and defeat dependence will emerge. The unresolved traumas will be processed thanks to the coping capabilities, which emerged during the EMDR sessions and the desensitization of the factors triggering the compulsion. This was demonstrated by the scores of the control scales: VOC and SOUTH defined in the first chapter. In summary, the first one shows the changes in the level of change of beliefs and starts from the value "1" up to the value "7". As the patient and therapist ascend, towards "7", they record the positive change in the related beliefs. The SOUTH scale, on the other hand, is used to measure the degree of anxiety or discomfort experienced. Starting from 0 "No disturbance", up to 10, "The maximum disturbance". The change in value from 10 to 0, experienced by the patient during treatment, is significant of improvement. From the clinical cases cited in the thesis work, this progress is evident. The safe place technique, a necessary principle in the EMDR protocol, will allow patients to find harmony and peace of mind with themselves and with others.

Analysis of natural disasters: The Earthquake

Natural disasters can be divided into 3 main categories:

1. hydro-meteorological disasters (such as overflows, storms, extreme temperatures)

2. biological disasters (epidemics, infestations)

3. geophysical disasters (earthquakes, tidal waves, volcanic eruptions)

Earthquakes have been responsible for the most devastating catastrophes of the 20th century, they occur suddenly, causing a violent and unexpected impact and the effects often last for a long time.

Psychological discomforts can be caused, in the survivors, as a consequence of displacement, i.e. the forced displacement due to the inability to use one's own homes, to the reconstruction of the same and to the relocation in an extraneous context that can lead to a disintegration of the social network.

All this makes us understand how from this situation is quite likely the onset of a PTSD (post-traumatic stress disorder), depressive disorder, substance abuse, sleep disorders, depressive disorder and anxiety disorders. Analysis of risk factors in the development of post-traumatic psychological distress:

greater exposure to the earthquake, proximity to the epicenter, the disintegration of the social network, a past history of trauma or emotional problems, financial losses, particularly affecting women, people with low levels of education, the lack of valid social support and displacement.

Many people affected by this natural traumatic event tend to seek help from General Practice services rather than specific psychological interventions in Mental Health services as a result of the fact that they tend to overlook the traumatic history experienced and ignore the mental problems resulting from the event.

The 4 phases following a natural disaster:

1. Heroic phase: people and the community try in every way to be able to help others and the community itself. Subjects can reach high levels of stress. It is therefore useful to remember not to underestimate the extent of this phenomenon even on themselves.

2. Honeymoon phase: we analyze the improvements and the number of people who have offered their help so as to generate a sense of common optimism. You don't have to

but underestimate the physical and especially psychological consequences that this event leaves in people.

3. Disillusionment phase: awareness of the extent of the event and its long-term effects emerges. The recovery will be long and difficult, but we must not be discouraged for this reason. It is at this time that clear symptoms of post-traumatic stress, irritability and the feeling of not receiving the necessary help may emerge. The suggestion is not to remain alone but to strengthen one another within the community and ask for the help of professionals.

4. Phaedrus-establishment   : Long-term returns balance

The EMDR technique was developed specifically for the treatment of TDS and can now be used to treat various disorders such as anxiety, phobias, recent trauma, excessive grief related to bereavement or to address the psychological aspects related to somatic diseases such as AIDS and cancer.

Initially this technique was called EMD or Eye Movement Desensitization, because it was born from a behavioral orientation and because it was thought that eye movements were specific in trying an effective desensitization. The effects of the treatment were to reduce the fear and anxiety associated with the trauma.

It was later discovered that other forms of bilateral stimulation (such as hand drumming and auditory stimuli) were equally effective.

The changes in the perception of anxiety and fear and the process of desensitization were the product of the re-elaboration of the individual's experience.

The treatment consisted in modifying body sensations and emotions from negative to positive, emerging the deepest insights and appearing in a completely spontaneous way new behaviors along with a new sense of self.

In this way the trauma is processed, and the person returns to feel a healthy and serene individual.

In this way the EMD acquires an additional component, "Reprocessing", becoming the current and well-known EMDR technique.

According to the first clinical reports in which the technique was applied, patients treated with EMDR showed a remission of symptoms related to the traumatic event already after a short number of sessions or even with just one session. Despite this, the first criticisms of this therapy were not long delayed, in particular the EMDR method and its supporters were accused of not having shown valid empirical results on the functioning of its most characteristic component, the eye movements.

The absence of a clear and consistent explanation of this component has led many scholars to consider EMDR as a simple alternative treatment to cognitive-behavioral exposure therapies.

Despite countless initial criticisms, various laboratory studies have shown the effectiveness of this technique centered on the movement of the eyeballs in terms of reducing negative emotions, vividness of images and attentive flexibility.

Neurobiological studies have highlighted the changes that occurred before and after EMDR surgery, along with a remission of trauma symptoms.

The EMDR treatment is based on the movements of the eyeballs, the aim is to stimulate, through the movement of the eyes, the amnestic networks in which the traumatic event has been isolated, connecting them to other autobiographical memories, thus restoring the normal path of information processing.

In this way the event experienced as disturbing can be integrated.

The work with EMDR focuses on remembrance that takes advantage of the natural adaptive information processing system. All this takes place in a guided and protected situation, which keeps away the risk of re-traumatization. His intervention is based on disturbing memory to reactivate and complete the interrupted processing.

Thanks to the intervention of bilateral stimulation, or even in some cases to the help of the therapist, the material blocked in the neural networks can be explored and reconnected to the rest of the information available to the brain. This link reactivates the processing, using the natural adaptive information processing system of our brain. In this way, negative beliefs, emotions and bodily sensations that had remained implicitly in the brain are made available, aware and integrated with the whole system.

The EMDR technique focuses on distancing the traumatic image making it less invasive, emotionally charged and vivid from the first treatment session. This is done thanks to the task of attention divided between the eye movements and the simultaneous exposure to the traumatic image. It is precisely in this that EMDR differs from the classic exposure therapies that tend to revive the patient's traumatic image in all its emotional intensity.

EMDR treatment steps
The treatment of EMDR consists of 8 phases: history and therapeutic planning, preparation, assessment, desensitization, installation, body scan, closure, re-evaluation.

The number of sessions per phase and the number of phases that can be addressed in each session varies greatly from patient to patient. Initially, the therapist explains to the patient the theory on which the EMDR is based and assesses whether the eyes of the latter can support the efforts required by the therapy, otherwise alternative techniques of bilateral stimulation such as rhythmic tapping on the hands or snapping of fingers near the ears are provided, even if they have not shown the same effectiveness as eye movements.

The two-finger therapist will produce movements to be followed by the patient (usually the distance between the two is 30-35 cm) in a direction that can be horizontal, vertical, diagonal or eight. Normally 24 right-left-right hand movements are sufficient.

During the sessions it is possible that the patient loses his capacity for self-control and emotional stability, so the therapist can propose the exercise of the "safe place": to make the patient imagine a place or a situation that allows him to relax and regain the feeling of self-control. In this way, the patient can interrupt the stress on the eyeballs and distance himself from the processing of the information, which is too disturbing for him at this time.

The metaphor of a running train is used, very illustrative to make the patient understand what he should feel:

"Imagine you're on a train and looking at the landscape that flows. Just note the landscape without trying to hold it back or make it meaningful. Remember that if you need to take a break, you just have to raise your hand." Once the preparation for EMDR therapy has been completed, the patient is asked to focus his or her attention on an image that represents the traumatic event. In the next phase of desensitization, the patient should keep in mind the image identified in the previous phase and follow the movement of the therapist's fingers. This movement will be repeated until the patient returns to the Subjective Units of Disturbance (SUD) scale, an 11-point Likert scale, which ranges from a neutral level of anxiety (0) to the maximum imaginable distress level (10), a value of 0 or 1.

In the event that other disturbing images emerge, the therapist is required to repeat the assessment and desensitization. We now move on to the phase of installing the positive cognition agreed in assessment. At the same time as the eye movement sets, the patient has to consider the target image and the desired positive cognition and thus free himself from the disturbing images. This knowledge must reach a level of 6 or 7 on the VOC scale (Validity of Cognition, a 7-point Likert scale ranging from "completely false" (1) to "completely true" (7)). If at this moment a new positive cognition appears, which he perceives as better than the previous one, the therapist is obliged to continue the installation phase with the new cognition more adaptive.

The body scan phase is thus reached. Always at the same time as the eyeballs are stimulated, the patient must mentally explore his body in search of physical sensations, rigidity or tensions that may emerge keeping in mind the target image and the positive cognition previously acquired. When the patient explores his body without finding more residual tensions, this phase can also be considered finished (cf. Shapiro, 1995).

The EMDR session ends with the closure phase, leaving the patient in a state of well-being and emotional stability.

The therapist teaches the patient how to manage any distress that may emerge between sessions, in addition to repetition of the metaphor of the train you can advise the patient to write down in a diary images, knowledge, feelings and disturbing emotions.

All these new stresses will be taken up again in the next EMDR session, and in particular in the re-evaluation phase the therapist will have to evaluate the presence of new targets to work on and evaluate the effectiveness of the processing obtained from the previous session.

EMDR therapy therefore allows the patient to distance himself from the image of the disturbing event, making it less invasive, emotionally charged and vivid from the first session.

The distance between the eyes is achieved thanks to the task of attention divided between the eye movements and the simultaneous exposure to the traumatic image, thus differing from the classic exposure therapies that focus on reviving the patient's traumatic image in all its emotional intensity.

The patient can distance himself from the disturbing images also thanks to the therapist's instructions to stay away from the traumatic images (metaphor of the train).

EMDR efficiency cases in environmental disaster situations

On August 17, 1999, Turkey and in particular the population of the areas surrounding the Sea of Marmara were hit by a powerful earthquake of magnitude 7.6 at 03:01:40 (local time), with a duration of 37 seconds.

This event killed over 25,000 people. The consequences on the mental health of the population were considerable.

Only two days after this earthquake, members of the Turkish Psychologists' Association (TPA) met to implement a program of psychotherapeutic intervention to deal with the situation. From the outset it was evident that many subjects had developed a post-traumatic stress disorder, which was confirmed by a study conducted the following year by the TPA-Istanbul Branch (TPA-IB) on 240 randomly selected families. Of all these, 70% suffered from TDPS.

To address the situation, TPA members worked for the creation of clinics in the tent camps, which provided therapeutic services to about 4000 people, including about 1500 individuals with symptoms of post-traumatic stress disorder.

Brochures describing the psychological effects of trauma were also published in order to make people aware of the possible consequences of this natural catastrophe and how to deal with them.

It soon emerged that despite the great help and support offered by the clinics in the tent camps, it was necessary for voluntary therapists to have more knowledge and more specific therapeutic training. Above all, specific difficulties emerged in the treatment of patients with posttraumatic nightmares, flashbacks, hyperarousal and avoidance symptoms.

As a result of this situation, it was decided to start a specific training programmed. Debriefing proved to be an inconsistent intervention technique if not aggravating the emergence of the TSPD, so other techniques have been studied.

Only the EMDR technique and cognitive-behavioral therapy (CBT) have brought benefits to patients with symptoms of post-traumatic stress disorder, these studies were conducted by the International Society for Traumatic Stress Studies. In fact, considering the specific and persistent conditions found daily in the tents of cities and especially because of the high level of chaos, cognitive-behavioral therapy was considered inadequate. Often the sessions took place in extremely crowded tent camps that exposed the subject to the gaze and listening of others, so much so as to limit it in recognizing its own level of anxiety and weakness. The survivors tended to suppress and suffocate the components that were most painful for them rather than requiring psychotherapy.

The main component on which the CBT method was based, the focus on the subject's exposure to the memories of the traumatic event, was considered a further inadequate element for a population that had suffered loss and substantial material loss.

Given the inadequacy of the techniques previously analyzed, the TPA commission introduced the EMDR technique, considered to be a better response to the dramatic situation of the Turkish population that survived the earthquake.

EMDR did not require the recording of the details of the traumatic experience, nor the assignment of homework as did cognitive-behavioral therapy.

The president of the TPA-IB made sure that the Turkish therapists started a training program on this technique.

Method

In January 2001, 167,000 people were able to take advantage of temporary accommodation in the earthquake zones. From now until June of the following year, clinical interviews and the PTSD Symptom Scale Self-Report (PSS-SR) diagnosed post-traumatic stress disorder in all people who had used the therapy.

These subjects were assigned to one of five therapists.

From the study it was decided to eliminate all those subjects who in the initial interview had shown signs of psychosis, dissociative disorders and those who showed a potential danger both for themselves and for other people.

After this screening process 58 patients were enrolled in three tent camps considered representative of the entire area affected by the earthquake in terms of the extent of deaths and injuries, structural damage, socio-economic disruption, population density and other variables that could have affected the trauma.

Ten subjects decided to leave the study before they had even completed their therapy (after three sessions), while seven others decided not to undergo the PSS-SR even though they completed the therapy.

Of the 41 participants who completed the PSS-SR post-treatment, 31 were women (aged 20-69, M = 43.32) and 10 men (aged 19-74, M = 41.20).

Of all these subjects, 21 were available and available for follow-up.

Designing

Due to the condition of the tent camps it was not possible to conduct a randomized controlled trial, but it was decided to apply a treatment in two different timeframes. Therefore, the participants were divided into "early-treated" (the first 50% of the participants in the treatment between January and July 2001) and "late-treated" (the last 50% of the patients treated between August 2001 and June 2002). These groups were compared to the PSS-SR scores.

Less educated subjects were more prone to the effects of traumatic events.

All participants were divided into 4 levels of education (5 years of schooling or less, 6-8 years, 9-12 years and more than 12 years of schooling).

11 participants with symptoms of TDD were already taking psychotropic drugs. Given the psychological conditions and the situation they were experiencing, the therapists decided not to exclude these subjects from the treatment sample, but their results were analyzed separately.

Instrumental evaluation

The PSS-SR is the self-report version of the structured PSS interview of post-traumatic stress disorder. It consists of 17 items that correspond to the symptoms described in the DSM-IV, so a diagnosis of the disorder can be obtained from the scores obtained at this scale of evaluation. The total score to the PSS-SR is obtained by adding the scores obtained to the different sub-scales of the test: Re-experiencing (5 items), Avoidance (7 items) and Arousal (5 items).

The Turkish version of the PSS-SR has acceptable psychometric properties.

The PSS-SR was assigned to the participants during the first interview (pretreatment measure) and was proposed again immediately after the final therapeutic session (posttreatment measure) and at the follow-up (six months after the final therapeutic session). The Subjective Units of Disturbance (SUD) scale is an 11-point Likert scale, which ranges from a neutral level of anxiety (0) to the maximum level of distress imaginable (10).

The VOC (Validity of Cognition) scale is a 7-point Likert scale that goes from "completely false" to "completely false".

(1) to "completely true" (7).

The five therapists who were involved in the therapy had a specific training and all had been in contact with EMDR for at least 15 months.

Procedure

Therapists began EMDR sessions in 90-minute sessions with an interval of 11.1 days between sessions. Each subject was asked to see the most painful image associated with the earthquake they had just suffered.

It was thought that it was necessary, with a traumatic event of this magnitude, to work on more than one disturbing image in order to eliminate the symptoms of post-traumatic stress disorder.

The EMDR treatment was performed in accordance with the 8-phase protocol proposed by Francine Shapiro.

In the first phase each participant was asked to depict themselves as the most disturbing image of the earthquake they had been victims of, this image would be the focus of the 3-8 sessions of the EMDR treatment.

Almost all participants in the experiment were given bilateral eye stimulation through the movement of the therapist's fingers. For those subjects (less than 10%) who had difficulty following the bilateral movement of their fingers, the stimulation was performed through the method of tapping (also called "tapping") on the patient's hands.

Once the treatment on the image considered by the patients as the most disturbing, the next images were passed, in a decreasing way on the basis of the emotional impact caused on the patient, obtaining for each of them a different score to the pre and post treatment SOUTH and VOC. The therapy could be considered completed when the participants obtained a score of 0 or 1 on the SOUTH scale for traumatic images and when the memory of the earthquake no longer produced painful emotions.

Results
Therapeutic experience

No differences emerged between the average scores obtained at the PSS-SR scale by patients treated by more experienced therapists, compared to less experienced therapists ($F (1, 19) = 0.24$, $p > .05$).

All participants, regardless of the therapist's experience with the EMDR method, showed a significant change over time both to the total score of the PSS-SR scale ($F (2, 38)$

$= 104.25$, $p < .01$), and in the three underwriters:

* Re-experiencing: $F (2, 38) = 72.20$, $p < .01$

* Avoidance: $F (2, 38) = 74.36$, $p < .01$

* Arousal: $F (2, 38) = 71.83$, $p < .01$

Comparison with the control group

No differences were found between the first and last treated groups in the results of the scale collected before EMDR treatment (t value ranges between 1.00-1.51, $p > .05$).

Finally, the data collected in the early traded group obtained at the post-treatment evaluation (i.e. immediately after the end of therapy) were compared with the data collected in the late-treated group obtained before the beginning of therapy (in this way it was possible to check for the effect of spontaneous remission associated with the passage of time from the traumatic event). Also, in this case, significant differences emerged both in the total score and in the scores obtained in all the subscriptions of the PSS-SR.

Effects of treatment

For the 41 participants included in the sample, an average of 5.02 EMDR sessions were used to complete the therapy. The average time between pre and post treatment evaluation was 3.05 months. For the sub-sample that also performed the six-month follow-up, a repeated measurement ANOVA was conducted. The data are shown in Figure 2. As can be easily deduced from the results shown in the figure, a significant effect of the treatment has emerged (in the direction of a reduction in symptoms) both on the total score and in all the substations of the PSS-SR instrument ($F(2, 40) = 105.33$, $p < .01$).

* Re-experiencing: $F (2, 40) = 75.69$, $p < .01$

* Avoidance: $F (2, 40) = 72.47$, $p < .01$

* Arousal: $F (2, 40) = 72.78$, $p < .01$

In particular, a positive effect of treatment was found in the comparison of pre- and post-treatment scores and in the comparison of pre-treatment and follow-up scores, but no significant differences were found between post-treatment and follow-up.

Using the PSS-SR criterion, 38 (92.7%) of the 41 participants who had been tested for pre-treatment did not exhibit PTSD at post-treatment. The three participants who continued, in accordance with the criteria of the PSS-SR instrument, showed at the post-treatment phase still a TDSD showed, however, a clear reduction of symptoms (in line with the average of the entire sample).

Number of images needed to complete therapy and changes in SOUTH and VOC scores

For the 41 patients enrolled, the number of images (memories) initially produced was 3.22 (Sd = 2.06). At the completion of the therapy, the average images were 2.2 (Sd = 1.27).

The resolution of the most disturbing memory required on average 2.87 sessions with a relatively high variability between subjects (range: 1-6).

This study, conducted in 1999 in Turkey, has allowed to gather empirical evidence in favour of the effectiveness of the EMDR technique in the treatment of post-traumatic stress disorder (PTSD) (through the use of the PSS-SR scale) in tent camps and has shown that the positive effects of remission were long-lasting.

Although the final sample consisted of only 41 subjects, the authors argue that these were representative of the 1500 people who were actually treated with the EMDR technique throughout the area affected by the earthquake.

In addition, the number of sessions (M = 5.02) and the effects of treatment were consistent with the data reported in the most rigorous randomized and controlled trials.

The authors finally point out that in the post-treatment phase there were significant differences in symptoms that were inversely related to the level of education of subjects, in this regard, the authors assumed that people with a lower level of education were more vulnerable to the effects of traumatic events in their lives due to lower economic and professional resources. In addition, the higher level of knowledge acquired through education can protect the individual against post-traumatic fears, a sense of lack of control and intrusive symptoms.

It is also important to note that the data from the comparison with the control group suggest that the reduction of anxious symptoms was due specifically to the EMDR treatment and not to a spontaneous remission associated with the passage of time.

The intervention programmed introduced by TPA following the 1999 earthquake in Turkey provides an example of how an intervention project following a major natural disaster can be carried out in a developing country. The authors conclude by hoping that this experiment can serve as a model of intervention to assist people affected by natural events or man-made disasters in other countries as well.

EMDR IN THE WORLD

Conference on "Earthquake and the Wounds of the Soul" The European community has increasingly recognized the importance of psychological interventions after a particularly dramatic collective event that damages the social fabric of a community.

It should be borne in mind that every earthquake can occur in a different way and the symptoms that occur in the population are varied, but one intervention technique that has proven effective in resolving symptoms in a short time has been that of EMDR.

Through these EMDR interventions on patients who were showing symptoms of post-traumatic stress, positive effects on the affected populations have been found, these interventions can also act as protection factors against subsequent shocks that may occur.

About 130 therapists were involved in the interventions to support the population of central Italy in a completely voluntary way.

The context of emergency is always associated with that of crisis, there is in fact a branch of psychology called "Psychology of disasters and crisis". The term "crisis" in reality has not only a negative connotation but can indicate a choice, decision and a condition of change necessary for the rearrangement of their lives.

Emergency psychology is not just about the individual but about the whole community. Following the events that took place on 24 August and 30 October, we can speak of a "collective disaster" in which the pain and trauma is not only found in the individual but also in the community and institutions. Anyone within a society is part of a system seriously affected and injured by the earthquake. The context in which one intervenes is that of deep uncertainty manifested by people, of reactions from stress, on physical health.

After the initial shock phase, the emotional impact emerges in all its pervasiveness.

The EMDR treatment therefore offered specific intervention tools to people who were experiencing the following symptoms:

* Intrusiveness: continuous images of the shocks, the roar and the sensory aspects related to the earthquake, intrusive thoughts, flashbacks.

* Avoidance: not always due to the unwillingness to talk about it, but in many people this symptom emerges because they do not succeed, they feel fear.

* Iperarousal: people still on the alert and frightened by sudden noises, are constantly stressed and cannot find a quiet.

* Depressed mood, persistent and negative thoughts, then comes the sense of abandonment, loneliness and fatigue when the rescuers will leave the affected areas and return to everyday life.

Many people as a result of this natural disaster have been forced to leave their territory of origin, their homes and their loved ones. This shift can sometimes block the processing of trauma, so people who have remained on the territory and who have benefited from psychological treatment are better able to deal with the situation and as far as possible return to normal in an easier way than people who had to leave their territory.

The lack of a safety period after a primary trauma such as a shock, is as if it did not allow people to enjoy a condition of tranquility and when another shock occurs the recovery becomes even more difficult.

By intervening with EMDR even in the peritraumatic phase it is possible that in people the arousal decreases.

* Norcia 1: from 26 August to 7 October (the center of the village had not yet been damaged) includes Norcia, Preci and Cascia. 42 EMDR therapists were involved, 18 psychologists of the Umbrian order conducted 443 triage evaluations. 576 EMDR interviews and the total number of people seen with EMDR were 256 plus 170 secondary school students. This data should take into account the total population of 5000 inhabitants.

In this phase the group EMDR was also conducted on students, USL officials, municipal officials, hospital operators, children with severe cognitive disabilities.

* Norcia 2: after 30 October. The damage was even more serious, and the population was re-traumatized. About 463 people were seen. Also, in this circumstance group treatments were conducted on children, nuns, students.

* Norcia 3: will be resumed at the end of January to finish the psychological contribution.

Some interventions have been made in neighboring countries but not directly affected by the earthquake such as Foligno, Terni, Fermo, Amandola.

As for the interventions on the city of Amatrice, since October 3, 14 therapists have intervened, the subjects visited were 59, of which 29 children, the request was made by the association "The Dawn of Small Steps".

In Fermo, about 1900 displaced persons were registered and 60 people were treated here by 17 therapists. In Teramo, interventions were requested on about 2000 students in schools.

In Amandola from 8 September to 3 October 88 people and 230 pupils were seen with whom the group EMDR was conducted on three different dates, that of 22 and 26 September and 1 October. The treatment follows standard procedures: the worst time is asked; the children draw it and from 0 to 10 must report their level of disorder. It was noted that these children started from a disturbance level of about 6 to reach 4 in a single group session of about 40 minutes. On September 26, in the same class, the initial discomfort is lower, starting from 4 we arrive at approximately 2. Finally, on the last date of October 1, starting from a value equal to 3, we reach a noise level of about 2.

So overall the discomfort has gone down.

The tools used in this first phase are: recent EMDR event protocol and group EMDR.

The goal is to help people achieve post-traumatic growth and thus transform an episode from negative to positive, increasing their ability to cope with critical events.

Several professionals n.e.c. (EMDR psychotherapists) highlighted how the setting in emergency contexts is distorted and consists of the relationship that the therapist creates in that situation with the traumatized subject who entrusts a part of his story to the therapist.

The target group can be varied, from a two-year-old child made by the same doctor to older people.

Network work is very important because if there were no relationship between civil protection, firefighters, red cross and psychologists there would be no effective clinical work and access to the large number of people to be treated.

Suffering is not only personal but also social/cultural and concerns the link with churches and symbolic buildings.

The emotional intensity that is created with the population as well as between colleagues is very strong.

Many operators, who personally intervened on the victims of the earthquake in central Italy and stressed the fact that the EMDR does not only intervene in post-traumatic conditions due to natural disasters, but in all those situations that can be traumatic for the subject as well as rapes, traumatic bereavement, suicides.

If there is an institutional activation (by the headmaster, the mayor, the civil protection, etc.), the EMDR offers its help and support completely free of charge.

The fundamental aspect to be taken into consideration in these contexts is that we intervene on people who before the catastrophic event led a normal life and without particular psychic symptoms of importance, who have a normal reaction to an abnormal event, which over time and without the therapeutic intervention could turn into DPTS. In this respect, the following are illustrated: (normal reactions to catastrophic events)

1. Fight: Fight

2. Flight: Escape

3. Freeze: hypertonic immobility, freezing

4. Faint: immobility in which the general mastery of the body is lost.

He also points out that from 24 to 72 hours following the trauma a shock phase can occur, it lasts a couple of hours and you can experience mental disorganization, confusion, loss of concentration. While only after this time window can feelings of guilt emerge.

Setting in emergency situations

In the emergency situation the setting loses its rigidity and can become any place, the interventions can be conducted in a tent city, in the open air. For example, the case of a lady victim of the earthquake who was treated in the open air, on wooden benches, is known because she had explicitly requested not to remain indoors. The lady was in the company of the doggie and at the time of the bilateral stimulation conducted by the therapist both followed the stimulation.

Specific protocols in case of emergency

There are two specific protocols for the emergency:

1. Group EMDR: has a structure made so that a group can have a treatment. Applied mainly in schools. The group can be of variable size, at least two experienced conductors are required, so that one conducts the group and the other can record the reactions of the participants. The groups are homogeneous, i.e. they are composed of people who have the same level of involvement in the trauma.

EMDR recent events

There are different levels of involvement in trauma:

- 1st type victims: it is the people who are directly affected by the event.

- 2nd type victims: relatives or loved ones of survivors or persons affected by the event.

- victims of type 3: rescuers and emergency workers.

- victims of type 4: community involved in the disaster.

- victims of type 5: people who, because of characteristics prior to the event, can react by developing a psychological disorder in the short or long term.

- 6th type victims: people who could have been first type victims or who feel involved for indirect reasons.

When working in an emergency, it is essential to conduct a "cascade of work", i.e. to work in a hierarchical sense. First of all, it is necessary to work on the rescuer in the event that he manifests symptoms of traumatization as a result of the situation because in these conditions he will not be able to help the users, i.e. the traumatized people. In fact, the rescuer can suffer a vicarious traumatization, even for non-direct exposure due to the traumatic conditions experienced on the spot and thus become primary victims. With rescuers can be conducted debriefing techniques.

We will then pass to the parent, if he shows clear symptoms of traumatization, for example he sleeps in a suit and is always alert to any noise, all this will pour on the child.

As for the victims, I am stratifying according to how much they were affected by the event. Therefore, the first step is to inform the population about the possibility of having this type of intervention. From 8 to 12 hours after you can do the defusing and between 24 and 72 hours you can do the debriefing, they are considered, unlike the EMDR of psychological supports conducted in groups and not of therapies. They are also conducted on the operators at the end of the shift. There must always be two experienced handlers on the psychology of emergency.

Direct experience

Following the seismic events that occurred in central Italy in August 2016, individual interventions were conducted in the Norcia area with the EMDR protocol for recent events and group interventions with middle school children and employees of the local health units. They were the therapists who moved to the tent camps.

In general, 3 to 6 sessions were necessary to process the single trauma (in line with the previous chapter).

People who had suffered the trauma had a greater sense of helplessness than a sense of guilt.

Obviously, the emotional response was influenced by several factors of protection or aggravating, such as the level of previous stress in the life of the subject, the degree of social support, the level of notice that there was.

The guidelines given to therapists of the association EMDR provides in case the activation of people is very high the selection of subjects involved through triage, is then administered the test with scale of impact of events, follows the safe place. So, after a short text part, conducted if the patient was not under shock, we start with the elaboration.

Previously unprocessed traumatic events:

In the two consecutive earthquakes of 24 August and 30 October in central Italy, it emerged that for some people the earthquake may have been an event that had not been worked out before, so the unresolved traumas of the 1979 or 1997 earthquakes were returning.

In this case with the standard event protocol you will need to work with the person on the previous event, once healed this will move to the recent trauma with the help of the recent event protocol.

Specifically, triage is the set of criteria on which the operator is based to make a classification of subjects in classes of treatment and to indicate the type of sending of the patient to health facilities that can heal his condition. The triage must make it possible to assess the psychological and psychiatric consequences of the catastrophic event, must be aimed in particular at victims, groups at risk and rescuers who are in difficulty in conducting the therapy in these emergency contexts. It is therefore necessary to pay attention to the way in which the evaluation is conducted, the context in which it is carried out, the needs and priorities expressed by the subject, the protection of privacy and the risk of stigmatization.

Trauma: medium and long-term consequences

The human being is a social animal, whose functioning is rooted in the nature of the social matrix in which it is inserted; from this it follows that the rupture or alteration of interpersonal relationships, which constitute this matrix, will have profound repercussions on both the biological and psychological functioning of the individual. This simple reflection is the basis for studies on the short- and long-term effects of trauma, which only recently have found a right of representation within the areas of investigation of contemporary psychopathology. A decisive contribution to the study of trauma and the origins of violence has been made by the psychology of object relations (Horner), Bowlby's attachment theory and Kohut's self-psychology; these authors have highlighted the importance of interpersonal relations, particularly early ones, in determining the way we perceive ourselves and relate to others. In 1980 the Post-Traumatic Stress Disorder (PTSD) was introduced into the DSM-III as an autonomous nosography entity; this gave further impetus to research into the relationships between traumatic events, short- and long-term reactions and psychopathology. In fact, as early as 1889, Pierre Janet had already dealt with post-traumatic reactions, describing dissociation as the main defensive mechanism used during trauma. Janet said that traumatized people are blocked and fixed to trauma, and unable to integrate traumatic memories, describing what is now called "procedural memory" in which information is stored in the form of sensations, emotions, not directly accessible to memory. He observed that these patients seemed to react to the memories of the trauma with emergency responses, which had been solicited during the original episode, but which were not related to the current event. Janet also noticed that the victims anchored in the trauma were unable to learn from experience because all their energies were directed at controlling emotions, to the detriment of paying attention to current needs. Janet actually described PTSD, but it was almost a century before the scientific community recognized this disorder as a real psychiatric condition and introduced it as an autonomous nosography entity.

Attention has since gradually shifted from the effects of discrete or major traumatic events to chronically traumatizing situations, which find their fulcrum in significant relational dynamics, particularly between the child and attachment figures. Being a victim of a traumatic experience involves emotions of fear and pain and the construction of a vulnerable self; these are precisely the basic conditions for the activation of the attachment system, which regulates the search for comfort in situations of danger throughout life. Attachment is one of the behavioral control systems that motivates the child to seek out and maintain, in dangerous situations, physical proximity to the reference figure in order to obtain protection. The attachment behaviors manifested by the child are the result of the quality of early interactions and determine the way in which the child processes the information. From the first year of life, also thanks to the child's development of cognitive/emotional/behavioral skills, attachment becomes a system of representations.

The Internal Operating Models. These mental models contain experiences and become a filter for reading reality. The Internal Operating Models, built on the basis of early experiences of attachment, are the reference criteria and give the subject the degree of confidence on the possibility of receiving care and protection appropriate to the requests. The attachment patterns identified by Mary Ainsworth (1978) are four: the avoidant attachment or "A", safe or "B", ambivalent or "C" and disorganized/disoriented or "D". The first three models identified (A, B, C) appear sufficiently finalized, coherent and integrated, the fourth (D) instead seems to be constituted by poorly finalized and apparently disorganized behavioral sequences. Pattern D is related to experiences of intense fear in interactions with significant attachment patterns. Recent studies have shown that the D pattern is present in 80% of children from abusive, neglected or disturbed family environments (Main, 1995). According to this author, the D model is an expression of the early effect of psychological trauma, since the central aspect that underlies it is the presence of a parent who, instead of providing a "safe basis" for the child's requests, is himself a reason for fear, either because he is abusing, or because he is unable to offer adequate care because he himself is in need of care. The D pattern has been proposed as an evolutionary precursor for the development of severe psychopathological disorders, such as borderline and dissociative ones (Liotti, 1995). The Internal Operating Models of the D pattern not only limit the subject's ability to seek protection when facing the emotional consequences of trauma but tend to amplify one of the consequences of this: fear.

Breaking attachment ties, or their deep inadequacy, can lead to serious consequences that damage both the ability to regulate affectivity, which the ability to use interpersonal relationships for modulating internal affective states.

The central feature of psychiatric patients with childhood trauma is the multiplicity of diagnoses and the variety of treatments they undergo, this is related to the extreme variability of the picture of symptoms: fear, depression, guilt, shame, anger, hostility, dissociative episodes, inappropriate sexual and eating behavior, are the symptoms that are frequently found among patients who are victims of abuse. Long-term consequences include poor impulse control, feelings of self-accusation, emptiness, low self-esteem and self-confidence, substance abuse, self-destructive behavior and eating problems.

In the cognitive-evolutionary perspective, the central psychological aspect of trauma is characterized by the loss of confidence that there is order and continuity in subjective experience. The presence of a secure internal or external base guarantees the possibility of controlling and understanding even those situations which, due to their complexity, exceed the subject's coping strategies. Trauma requires the individual to re-set the pre-existing mental structures, without destroying the sense of continuity and coherence of his own existence and therefore of his own personal identity. These capacities of resetting presuppose the development, in the first years of life, of adequate cognitive-affective patterns, which regulate the perception of oneself, of the other and of interpersonal relations. It is therefore understandable that "the earliest, and perhaps most harmful, form of psychological trauma is the loss of a safe basis" (van der Kolk, 1987).

Child sexual abuse. Introduction to the phenomenon. What can be the consequences?

Some longitudinal studies carried out in the 1980s have stimulated researchers to investigate the existence of a possible relationship between a history of traumatic experiences, and in particular physical abuse and sexual abuse, and the development of eating disorders.

The Council of Europe of 1986 proposed the following definition of "abuse": "Acts and deficiencies which seriously disturb the child, undermine the child's physical integrity, physical, intellectual and moral development, the manifestations of which are neglect and/or physical and/or psychological and/or sexual injury by a family member or others who care for the child".

The abuse is, therefore, considered as such, not only if it consists of real acts, but also by shortcomings in acts that socially and culturally, would expect to be carried out to ensure the children a normal physical and mental development.

The definition elaborated by CISMAI in the Declaration of Consent on child sexual abuse of 1999, says: sexual abuse "is the involvement of a child by a prominent partner in sexual activities even if not characterized by explicit violence. It is always and, in any case, configured as a confusing and destabilizing attack on the personality of the minor and on his evolutionary path".

Child sexual abuse is a traumatic experience that can prejudice the normal biological and psychological development of the individual; such childhood traumas leave a feeling of despair and shame that conditions the victim and forces him to isolate himself, to close in on himself, to deny trust to himself and others, to develop death impulses. The abuse in the child constitutes a cascade of Psychic events, which only have their origin in the trauma, but which come to develop later precisely to defend themselves from the intolerance of the trauma itself.

The existence of a specific and direct connection between sexual violence (or other traumatic experiences) and the subsequent development of an eating disorder has not yet been demonstrated. But both the existing research data and the clinical experience brought by the therapists working with these patients seem to lead to at least one general conclusion: the severe sexual and/or physical violence suffered during childhood and early adolescence puts the patient at particular risk of developing psychiatric disorders, including eating disorders.

In the field of scientific literature, in recent decades, there has been a rapid increase in the number of studies on this subject.

Studies on clinical samples

Oppenheimer, Howells, Palmer and Chaloner (1985) published the first large-scale study carried out on 78 outpatients, 70% of whom were found to have experienced sexual violence during childhood and/or adolescence. However, this research did not reveal any relationship between the history of violence and the type of eating disorder diagnosed.

Kearney-Cooke (1988) considered a sample of 75 bulimic women and found a history of sexual trauma in 58% of patients. The study by Root and Fallon, in the same year, found that out of a group of 172 patients with eating disorders, 65% had suffered physical abuse, 23% had been raped, 28% had been the victim of sexual violence during childhood and 23% had suffered maltreatment in their relationship.

Bulik, Sullivan and Rorty (1989) conducted research on sexual violence in childhood and on the family environment of 34 bulimic patients: 34% of the subjects in this sample had previously suffered episodes of violence. Steiger and Zanko (1990) in their study compared the prevalence of proven sexual violence in a group of 73 subjects with eating disorders and in two other control groups, one consisting of 21 psychiatric patients and the other consisting of 24 "normal" women. From this study it emerged that, among the women belonging to the group with eating disorders, about 30% reported having suffered sexual violence, compared to 33% of psychiatric patients and 24% of "normal" women. Within the group of patients with eating disorders, the percentage of those with "restrictive" anorexia who had experienced sexual violence was significantly lower (6%) than in the other groups.

Waller (1991, 1993a) examined 100 patients with eating disorders and found that 50% had been abused and the prevalence of violence found in this sample seemed to be associated with the diagnostic category: women with bulimic disorders reported higher rates of sexual experience than anorexic patients with restrictive type. The author later (1992a) showed that the frequency of binge eating and vomiting is much higher in women who report episodes of sexual violence with particular characteristics: that is, when the violence occurred within the family, it involved the use of force and occurred before the age of 14. Welch and Fairburn (1994), in a largely controlled study, observed four groups whose subjects were individually matched: 50 cases of bulimia nervosa belonging to the health care territory, 50 control subjects who were also part of the health care territory and without eating disorders, 50 control subjects affected by psychiatric problems and the and 50 patients hospitalized for bulimia nervosa. The period in which the episodes of violence occurred was established through an interview that took place in the house of each subject. The results showed a clear numerical prevalence, compared to the control group, of inpatient patients with bulimia nervosa who had been victims of sexual violence before the onset of their disorder: 26% compared to 10%. However, there was no difference in the rates of sexual violence between inpatient patients with bulimia nervosa and psychiatric patients in the control group (24%). The two authors of the research concluded that the violence suffered during childhood increases the risk of psychiatric disorders, and among those disorders includes bulimia nervosa.

The cat amnestic study conducted by Gleaves and Eberenz (1994) showed that in eating disorders the presence of sexual violence could be related to an unfavorable prognosis. The authors studied a sample of 464 bulimic women being treated in a residential facility for women with eating disorders and examined the correlation between history of sexual violence and symptoms suggesting an unfavorable prognosis, as in the case where the patient had received different treatments and hospitalizations, or had manifested self-injuring behavior or carried out suicide attempts and drug addiction problems. The results showed that among patients who showed all symptoms for an unfavorable prognosis, about 71% reported a history of sexual violence, compared to 15% of the subjects in the sample who had no prediction factor of an unfavorable diagnosis.

Most of this research has focused on the incidence of sexual violence, but there are researchers who point to the need to analyses the full range of sexual violence.

Range of possible negative experiences of women with eating disorders. The bulimic women, compared to the others, reported higher levels of physical violence, psychological violence and multiple violence to which they had been subjected during childhood. The authors conclude by stressing how important it is, in the case of patients with eating disorders, to examine the full spectrum of possible experiences of violence, rather than focusing exclusively on sexual violence.

Studies on non-clinical samples

Calam and Slade (1989) administered questionnaires to a group of 130 university students: 20% of these girls reported having had unwanted sexual experiences before the age of 14 and, in 13% of these cases, it was intra-family abuse. The experience of sexual episodes in which force was used was associated with abnormal eating attitudes and behaviors. But only undesired sexual intercourse before the age of 14 had a significant correlation with bulimic tendencies. Bailey and Gibson (1989) studied the possible relationship between bulimia nervosa and experiences of violence in a group of 294 university students: 13% said they had been sexually harassed during childhood, 11% said they had been subjected to rape, 8% said they had been beaten and 6% said they had been physically abused. Only physical violence was significantly associated with the presence of bulimic symptoms.

Smolak, Levine and Sullins (1990) administered questionnaires to 298 university students: 23% of these reported having been sexually abused during childhood and, compared to the group that did not report any violence, had a greater number of symptoms related to eating disorders.

Kinzl, Traweger, Guenther and Biebl (1994) found, in a sample of 202 university students, an incidence rate of sexual violence of 21%, but found no difference, with regard to symptoms of an eating disorder or related characteristics, among women who had had had none, one or more episodes of violence. However, the study showed that girls who reported living in a difficult family environment had a higher incidence of diseases related to eating disorders. The authors concluded that violence at an early age is neither necessary nor sufficient for the subsequent development of eating disorders, while living in a difficult family environment can become an important etiological factor.

The study by Hastings and Kern (1994) focused on the presence of sexual violence and bulimia in a sample of 786 university students and on how this pathology could be linked to past family experiences. Their results seem to demonstrate that the experience of sexual violence combined with a chaotic family environment contribute to increasing the chances of onset of bulimia.

Presence of dissociative symptoms in eating disorders the traumatic event in children would overwhelm the processing skills of the child who is exposed to a situation of extreme physical suffering and from which she cannot escape and to which she can hardly react. In this case, the child will use the defensive mechanism of dissociation in order to cushion the suffering and to maintain an organized behavior, thanks to the lesser conscious perception of physical pain and the lesser or absent awareness of the event. The frequency of abuse will make it easier to use the dissociative mechanism even in the case of events with less traumatic violence, a sort of privileged defensive strategy. The absence of a caring adult will prevent the child from accessing the possibility of using language, which would facilitate in him the construction of a semantic memory integrated with the personal consciousness, thus keeping the episode or episodes in a space of consciousness not verbalized and dissociated.

In recent years, researchers have begun to systematically study the presence of dissociative symptoms in eating disorders.

Sanders (1986), author of a new scale to measure dissociation, the so-called PAS (Percentage Alteration Scale), demonstrated how university students who used to binge reported a higher degree of dissociative phenomena than control groups composed of normal girls.

Demitrack, Putnam, Brewerton, Brandt and Gold (1990) examined dissociative experiences in 30 patients with eating disorders, comparing them with 30 "normal" women who appeared to them by age; they found that patients had far higher levels of psychopathology than control subjects.

Herzog, Stoley, Carmody, Robbins and van der Kolk (1993) studied the presence of both sexual violence and dissociative symptoms in 20 patients with eating disorders: 65% of subjects reported sexual violence during childhood and patients with a higher degree of comorbidity reported this type of experience more often. Subjects with a history of violence scored significantly higher on one of the dissociation scales.

Berger et al. (1994) conducted a study in Japan on a sample of 41 outpatients suffering from eating disorders: this study showed that 45% of the total sample had suffered a combination of physical and sexual violence. Of these patients, 22% met the criteria for Multiple Personality Disorder (MPD) classification according to DSM-III-R and 15% had scores on the dissociation scale indicating a high probability of developing an MPD or PTSD.

Everill, Waller and MacDonald (1995) studied the link between dissociation and eating disorders in a clinical group of bulimic women and a non-clinical group of university students. In the non-clinical group, it was found that certain particular dissociative styles were linked to bulimic tendencies. In the group with eating disorders an association between scores on one of the dissociation scales and the frequency of binges emerged. The authors concluded that the presence of both symptoms, dissociative and bulimic, may suggest a history of early experiences of violence or stress, or a major loss.

From Grave, Rigamonti and Todisco (1995) in their study found the clear prevalence of dissociative symptoms in a sample of 103 patients with eating disorders, compared to the control group. 20% of women with eating disorders reported high levels of dissociative symptoms. In particular, a correlation between dissociation and eating disorders was found, especially in patients with a bulimic component.

Vanderlinden and Vandereycken (1993) investigated the relationship between traumatic experiences and dissociative phenomena in a group of 98 patients suffering from eating disorders, all diagnosed according to the criteria of the DSM-III-

R. Traumatic experiences were evaluated through a self-describing questionnaire on unwanted sexual episodes during childhood (Lange, Kooiman, Huberts and Van Oostendorp, 1995) and through clinical interviews; for the analysis of dissociative experiences they used the self-describing questionnaire DIS-Q (Dissociation Questionnaire). The DIS-Q is a self-descriptive scale made up of 63 items and four underclasses: (1) confusion of identity and fragmentation;

(2) loss of control; (3) amnesia; (4) absorption. In addition to sexual violence that could range from caresses to rape, the following situations were also taken into consideration because they were considered severely traumatic: physical abuse, complete emotional neglect or abandonment during childhood and loss of a close relative. Only traumatic situations that occurred before the onset of the eating disorder were evaluated. The overall incidence rate of trauma was 28%; 20% of patients reported sexual violence during childhood, which in 8% of cases was incestuous in nature. Patients with "mixed" anorexia nervosa, bulimic patients and patients with atypical eating disorders had much higher rates of traumatic experience: 25%, 37% and 58% respectively compared to restrictive anorexia (12%). The incidence of sexual violence was significantly lower in the last group (only 3%) than in the other three subgroups with eating disorders (20%). These data therefore demonstrate the existence of a relationship between the presence of a traumatic experience and the type of food pathology. Subjects who had been sexually assaulted reported the highest scores in the DIS-Q, particularly in the under-stairs of amnesia. The latter has proved to be the most specific feature that distinguishes patients who have suffered sexual violence from those who have not. In DIS-Q about 12% of the sample with eating disorders reported experiences of dissociation at the same level as a group of patients with dissociative disorders. These

data suggested that dissociative experiences related to trauma could play an important role in a subgroup of patients with eating disorders, particularly bulimic behavior.

Some mediation factors

The Declaration of Consent on child sexual abuse elaborated by CISMAI in 1999 states about the consequences of sexual abuse: "The intensity and quality of the harmful outcomes derive from the balance between the characteristics of the event (earliness, frequency, duration, severity of sexual acts, relationship with the abuser) and factors of protection (individual resources of the victim, his family environment, activated interventions in the psychosocial, health, judicial). Consequently, the damage is all the greater the more: the phenomenon remains hidden or is not recognized; protection is not activated in the primary context and in the social context; the experience remains unwritten and unprocessed; the relationship of dependence of the victim with those who deny the abuse is maintained".

Clinical experience confirms that some parameters can play an important role in the different definition of phenomena resulting from child sexual abuse. It has been hypothesized that other factors may constitute elements of interference or mediation between the input constituted by trauma and the output constituted by psychopathology. These mediation factors must also be evaluated in the diagnostic path and can provide the therapist with valuable information to plan the treatment.

Numerous studies have shown that there is a link between the age at which violence first occurred and its consequences. The age of the victim is inversely related to the severity of the psychopathological damage suffered: in general, the younger the child is, the greater the effect of the trauma. This consideration can be explained by assuming that the lower the age at which violence occurs, the more primitive the defense mechanisms activated by traumatic experience will be. Human responses to psychic trauma include psychological and behavioral hyperactivity (state of overexcitation, flashbacks and nightmares), accompanied by loss of sensitivity (social isolation, sense of alienation, anhedonia). Humans, when confronted with trauma at an early age, react as if they were immobilized, caught by paralysis. Such a reaction is typical of animals when they find themselves in situations that threaten their lives. According to Nijenhuis and Vanderlinden (1995) the analogy between human and animal defenses can also be extended to the typical behavior of prey animals that change their eating patterns when they feel the danger. In these circumstances they become nervous and show a prolonged abstinence from food, interrupted by a short and rapid ingestion of large quantities. Very young children, in addition to the stiffening reaction and food changes, have few or no other defensive mechanisms to react to impending traumatic experiences.

The modalities of abuse are relevant: the sexual act obtained with aggressiveness and violence is different from the one obtained with subtle tenderness for the child. Calam and Slade (1989) showed that women with eating disorders were more likely to experience unwanted, forced sexual experiences than women in control groups. It is therefore essential to investigate the specific details of the violence, such as the type of contact that has taken place, the degree of threat or whether force has been used, the frequency and duration of the violence itself. It is also different, in its psychopathological consequences, the abuse perpetrated within the home by a parent or brother, compared to that suffered by acquaintances or strangers. Intra-familiar sexual abuse, unlike most traumas, interpersonal and nonpersonal, is characterized by having the source of trauma in a person who, on the contrary, should provide containment, reassurance and help in overcoming the traumas themselves. This is particularly true when the abuser is a parent, in which case the abuse, besides being a trauma in itself, tends to significantly interfere in the development of the attachment's behavioral system. According to Calam and Slade (1989), intra-family abuse is associated with anorexia nervosa "with low body weight", because "self-reducing hunger could serve to punish the parent who exploited it instead of protecting it".

The revelation of violence and the response the victim received seem to be important mediating factors between violence and its subsequent psychological consequences. Everill and Waller (1995) by examining a sample of patients with eating disorders demonstrated that the reaction of family members to the revelation of violence contributes to the formation of psychopathological disorders of adulthood. Waller and Ruddock (1993) discovered that the patient's perception of a lack of response or a hostile response was related to certain symptom patterns, in particular the frequency of vomiting and symptoms of Borderline Personality Disorder.

Family variables can play an important mediating role in determining the general level of psychological difficulties of adulthood. Family studies have shown that anorexics with a bulimic component report more conflict and disorganization in the family environment than restrictive anorexics. Schmidt, Tiller and Treasure (1993) wanted to investigate whether childhood experiences and the quality of care received at the same time in life had an effect on the course of eating disorders. In this research they examined, through semi-structured interviews, the family environment of the childhood of four groups of patients. The variables taken into consideration were parental indifference, parental control, intra-family disagreements and intra-family violence. Research showed that normal-weight bulimic women reported higher levels of parental indifference and excessive control, physical abuse and violence against other family members than restrictive anorexics. In general, these results suggest that negative episodes of life, combined with unfavorable family experiences, may influence the course of the disease; patients with a bulimic component reported more negative events experienced during childhood than patients with anorexia nervosa. Vandereycken (1994) conducted studies on the role of parental function in eating disorders; from the results it appears that bulimic patients have a particular family pattern. These patients report having grown up in an environment characterized by a lack of attention on the part of their parents and in particular on the part of their mother. Mothers are perceived as negligent and unreliable, while fathers are considered to be overprotective but without proof of affection. Therefore, a pathological form of parental function or a distorted perception of it can be considered as a peculiarity of a more general negative atmosphere within the families of bulimic patients. Selvini Palazzoli (1981) states that in anorexics there would be a denial of stimuli coming from the body, and the refusal of food in such patients would be interpreted as a struggle for power to win the individual battle for existence. By denying its dependence on others and assuming a role of power, anorexia would overturn the dynamics in which it has been inserted with abuse. From what emerged, it becomes essential to resort to the screening of past and present family experiences and dynamics, achievable through semi-structured interviews and/or questionnaires such as the Parental Bonding Instrument and the Leuven Family Questionnaire. Particular attention should be paid to chaotic, less cohesive and/or disorganized families that are often encountered when working with patients with eating disorders.

Another important factor is the self-image, i.e. the consideration that patients have of themselves. Victims of sexual and physical violence often have little self-esteem, a strong sense of guilt and shame (Herman, 1992; Jehu, 1988). Guilt, shame and self-pity are extremely frequent and decisive, including the tendency towards self-denigration, the conviction that one deserves nothing, that one has no power and that one is inferior. A negative self-image, based on self-pity, can be a mediating factor between input (trauma) and outcome (dissociative symptoms and eating disorders). The more girls blame themselves for the violence they have suffered, the greater the possibility that the experience of violence will be dissociated from their conscience. Girls with a negative self-esteem will either end up isolated from the group of peers or join more marginalized groups of young people with various problems.

The factors of mediation between the violence suffered in childhood (input) and subsequent psychological problems (output) are obviously related in many respects and will vary considerably from person to person. Vanderlinden and Vandereycken (1997) have proposed a multifactorial model in which the sociopsychological adaptation of the victim of a trauma is represented along a continuum that goes from the constructive integration of the traumatic experience, to the bioadaptive dissociation that brings all kinds of related psychopathological symptoms. Whether the victim can integrate traumatic experiences into his or her conscious psychological life or whether he or she dissociates them will depend on a combination of all these factors.

CONCLUSIONS

Sometimes a walk in a park is enough to make a discovery that changes the rules of the game. This is the case of desensitization and reworking through eye movements (EMDR).

Sometimes a walk in a park is enough to make a discovery that changes the rules of the game. This is the case of desensitization and reworking through eye movements (EMDR), a psychotherapeutic method recently invented that allows you to rework the traumas of the past, but also to manage the problems related to anxiety and to strengthen the security of their individual resources.

Born from an apparently random observation, the EMDR approach is now a safe and effective technique for the treatment of a wide range of disorders, ranging from those related to anxiety - including phobias and social anxiety - to those characterized by summarizing or obsessive-compulsive symptoms, but also addictions, eating disorders, depression, acute bereavement and so on.

The important thing is to turn to competent people: the EMDR treatment is delicate and complex and requires technical skills and emotional management skills, to be found exclusively in the figure of the psychotherapist (it is not enough to the psychologist or counsellor) who has undergone a specific training and recognized at specialized centers.

Made in the USA
Monee, IL
27 December 2023

50600279R00057